MW00780039

TAKING THE
MOUNTAIN
of EDUCATION

A Strategic Prayer Guide
to Transform American Schools

Nancy Huff

Unless otherwise indicated, all scripture quotations are taken the Holy Bible, New International Version®, NIV®. Copyright © 1973, 1978, 1984 by Biblica Inc.™ Used by permission of Zondervan. All rights reserved worldwide. www.zondervan.com.

Scripture quotations marked KJV are taken from the *King James Version* of the Bible.

Scripture quotations marked NKJV are taken from the New King James Version. Copyright © 1982 by Thomas Nelson Inc. Used by permission. All rights reserved.

10 9 8 7 6 5 4 3 2 1

Taking the Mountain of Education by Nancy Huff
ISBN: 978-0-692-26858-2
Copyright © 2014 by Nancy Huff
Printed in the United States of America

All rights reserved. None of this book may be reproduced or transmitted in any form or by any means, electronic or mechanical, including photocopying, recording or by any information storage and retrieval system, without the written permission of the publisher. Printed in the United States of America.

To my husband Keith
for years of encouragement,
love and support.

I was blessed reading your book! **It is AWESOME! It is BRILLIANT! It is DYNAMITE!** *You watch and see what* **God** *does with this book! This* **Mountain** *is coming down!*

Everyone knows that we have problems in our schools, but I for one did not know the **true history** *of the plans and schemes that our adversary Satan, has used over many years! Your book is a book of* **truth!** *The Bible says that* **"We shall know the truth and the truth shall set us free!"**

Thank you for hearing God's call to write this book, and your perseverance and hard work in bringing it to fruition! I know that our Father is saying: "Well done my beloved daughter!"
Rich Eldred

Nancy Huff and her book, **Taking the Mountain of Education** *are answers to a lot of our prayers. We all want the best education for our children and grandchildren, and we all want our American Schools to be transformed, and this book has the best strategies to accomplish it that I have ever seen.*

Nancy is the leader for the Heartland Apostolic Prayer Network (HAPN) for transformation of education of our nation (we call it the "Education Mountain")

HAPN has a leader and a prayer network in all 50 states and 57 nations (I am the founder and overall leader). C. Peter Wagner says that HAPN has "the most tangible, measurable results of high level prayer and spiritual warfare that I have heard yet in my life". We have been asking God for wisdom and revelation on how to get tangible, measurable results in transforming the Education Mountain, and Nancy and her book are great answers to our prayers. Ephesians 6:12 says that our real struggle is in the unseen realm against demonic forces. **Taking the Mountain of Education** *is a tremendous help in identifying what and where those forces are, how and when they go there, and what to do about them. I thank God for Nancy and this book, because we are getting some real, tangible breakthroughs in prayer and spiritual warfare across our nation and fully expect it to continue.*

If you really want to make a lasting difference in the education system of our nation, buy the book and do what it says. You will be so glad you did!

Dr. John Benefiel, Founding Leader of the Heartland Apostolic Prayer Network

Thank you so much for your book! I'm getting ready to share it with the HAPN Executive Leadership Team in California this weekend. I just love all the history, the repentance, prophetic declarations and the locations we should go to for prayer. This is going to be an awesome tool for dealing with the Education Mountain and I sincerely appreciate all that you did in compiling it.

Audrey Pannier, California Executive Leadership Team

Table of Contents

ACKNOWLEDGMENTS

I thank God continually for Victory Christian Center in Tulsa, OK and for my Pastors Billy Joe and Sharon Daugherty. They continually cast a clear vision to reach out to people with the Love of Jesus. Even though Pastor Billy Joe is no longer on this earth, he lives on in the vision he imparted to each one of us who sat under his teachings. Pastor Sharon has done an excellent job of steadying the ship and loving us all.

Apostle John Benefiel gave me the encouragement needed to finish this book. He introduced me to a group of world changing, transformational prayer warriors at Heartland Apostolic Prayer Network for which I am extremely grateful.

To Drs. Mark and Betsy Neuenschwander who found me as a "beached whale" and pushed me back into the ocean to impact the nations.

To all the friends of Teach the Children International who gave, so this book could be published. They are the real heroes as they have stood by me for years.

A special thanks to Rich Eldred for his patiently reading the manuscript and giving me wonderful suggestions to improve the message.

Nancy Huff

1 Creating a Safe Place to Learn

Heavy metal music pulsed like hearts on steroids as 18-year-old Eric Harris and 17-year-old Dylan Klebold worked on another after-school project. For a long time their extra-curricular activities had included creating an online website to host the video game *Doom*. Gifted boys, they'd moved on to something m ore challenging: mass murder.

For a year they'd spent every waking moment planning an event that they hoped would rival the Oklahoma City bombing. They built a fire bomb to draw fire fighters away from Columbine High School. They converted two propane tanks to bombs, built 99 explosive devises, and rigged bombs in two cars. They collected a stockpile of guns, sawing off the barrels to make them easier to hide.

On Tuesday, April 20, 1999, Eric and Dylan were busy before school. They hid a firebomb in a field three miles away, which was set to detonate at 11:14 a.m. Just before lunch, they placed two duffel bags in the cafeteria where they were lost amid hundreds of backpacks. Inside each duffle bag they'd placed propane bombs rigged to detonate at 11:17 a.m.

With everything in place, the boys waited at their cars with enough ammunition to kill everyone who tried to escape—and any rescue workers who tried to get inside. When the cafeteria bombs failed to explode, they went inside and began shooting.

By 11:35 a.m., terrified students realized that the boys were getting bored with killing their victims with guns. "Maybe we should start knifing people!" Klebold said. "That might be more fun!" Instead, they threw a Molotov cocktail at the unexploded propane bomb in the cafeteria. It detonated, igniting a fire.

Before committing suicide, Eric and Dylan murdered 24 students, one teacher, and left countless wounded. The death rate paled in comparison to the Oklahoma City bombing, but the shock left the whole world reeling.

I was one of millions of Americans who wept as the events that day played out across television screens. I'd spent my entire adult life in the education system. As an algebra teacher, I thought I'd seen it all. But nothing had prepared me for the senseless murders of so many children.

Of course, Eric Harris and Dylan Klebold made their own choices. They are ultimately responsible for all the horror of that day. But I had an uneasy feeling that it would be a mistake to shake our heads at the cruelty of two depressed and psychopathic teens. We had to take a deeper look at an education system so toxic that it might well be incubating them.

I was not only a teacher but an intercessor called to pray for our educational system. This was the worst kind of wake-up call for America and I knew that we couldn't afford to sleep through the alarm. I realized that we were never going to change this nation without changing the environment for our children. To do that, we have to learn our lessons from the past, plan, implement, and carry out strategic spiritual warfare that targets the root of the problem.

This book is that battle plan.

It was two weeks after the Columbine massacre when I attended an impromptu meeting in Littleton, Colorado, so that people living in the aftermath of the tragedy could share their feelings and somehow find a measure of peace. Clearly they would never be the same.

As I expected, God in His faithfulness had warned many people of the danger. Like so many Christians in the Church today, they didn't know what to do with the information. Who should they tell? Was there a clearing house for such information? How should they pray? These were the same questions a lot of us from Oklahoma had asked in the shadow of the Oklahoma City bombing.

One minister said, "I knew something was going to happen at this school and I knew it would be devastating, but I didn't know what. I just knew in my spirit."

"Every day when I saw the boys dressed up totally in black Gothic coats and acting all weird, I knew they were going to kill someone," a teenager admitted. "I just didn't know when."

"I felt in my spirit that something was going to happen at this school," another minister said. "Don't ask me how. I just knew. I'm so sorry that I couldn't have done something to prevent this tragedy."

Every speaker that day—parents, students and ministers—were Christians. Each shared his or her premonition and inner promptings by the Holy Spirit of impending danger. My heart ached as one after the other spoke about what they had seen or sensed in the spirit days, weeks, months and some even years before Eric Harris and Dylan Klebold walked into Columbine High School in Littleton, Colorado with a plan for mass murders.

As I listened, my spirit made a heart cry to God. "Lord, how do we pray for America's students? How do we raise up intercessors to stand in the gap before You for the students in the schools of our land?" There was a deep sense of emptiness in the pit of my stomach that stayed with me on the fourteen hour drive from Littleton back to Tulsa, Oklahoma.

That day changed my life forever and set me on a mission to find a comprehensive and effective way to pray for our schools and for the students in them. I spiritually mapped the American educational system by delving into our educational history in order to identify the spiritual forces behind the detrimental decisions some of our forefathers made that took us down the path of humanism. I identified the major spirit behind humanism as Baal, the same false god of the Old Testament that required child sacrifices. History revealed the entry points where Baal was allowed to enter our schools. At that point, prayer strategies were developed that would sever the root causes of humanism. My next objective was to raise intercessors who would engage in effective prayer for the America educational system.

Within these pages are the revelations I discovered that will help us pray with the spiritual insight necessary to create a reformation in our schools. It *is* possible to see our educational system changed.

This book will not tell you how to get more involved in schools, elect more Christians to local school boards, or how to provide more legal advice for Christian teachers. My organization, Teach the Children International, has done many of these activities, and while they are good things, they are a minute portion of what needs to be accomplished. We must go deeper to the roots of the causes of our problems and not spend all our time on manifestations of the enemy. We simply do not have time to pray surface prayers. America's schools and consequently our nation is on the brink of destruction and the sooner we realize it and take action, the better off we will be. By taking action, I mean instigating a positive strategic prayer movement that will change the Mountain of Education systemically.

Columbine was one of a series of wake-up calls. No matter how dark things look with our natural eyes, we as the Church have the answers, so we must take a stand. The first stand we have to take is in the arena of prayer. Let us put aside our fears and the burdens of our daily lives and engage ourselves in the war that is before us. This isn't the time to close our eyes to the situation and hope for the Rapture to rescue us. We know the Lord is on our side and we will surely win if we do not give up.

2 How Bad Is It?

One of life's greatest pleasures is to sit across the table from a friend and catch up on each other's lives. Recently I had that privilege with a friend who teaches at a nearby public school. We'd taught at the same school for many years and getting together with her was a treat. Excited about this book I told her, "Just think, this is a way to pray for education that will deal with the root causes of the problems we faced in the classroom."

I could tell she wasn't impressed. So I tried another approach that I hoped would pull out of her some deep wisdom about the root causes of America's educational woes. "Okay, you tell me what you think are the root causes for why our educational system is so bad and why we can't fix it," I said.

She leaned across the table toward me and replied, "I think it's the way we handle mainstreaming the special needs kids. Another thing is the amount of medications I have to dispense every day. Do you know that before I start teaching in the morning, I have to make sure that seven out of my twenty-three kids have visited the school nurse to take meds for ADHD? And there is the principal—she's new, doesn't know her job, and we are supposed to tell her every little thing."

She leaned back and threw up her hands. "How in the world are we supposed to teach?"

I took a deep breath and just looked at her. Our ideas on the root causes of educational problems were miles apart. I have to say, I have done enough classroom teaching to know that just trying to keep one's head above water is difficult and classroom management is an art that has to be learned and relearned almost daily. Teachers deal with classroom discipline that must be handled with little or no administrative assistance, student attendance is sporadic at best, administrators do not support the teachers, and the list goes on. Teachers are overwhelmed, as are administrators. Almost everyone in this country knows that our educational system needs an overhaul, but they don't know what to do about it. Things are about as bad as they can get, and not getting any better. Yet the powers in control of education continue to go along the path of destruction.

And this is just the tip of the iceberg. Thomas Sowell, a nationally syndicated columnist and Senior Fellow on Public Policy at the Hoover Institute, Stanford University and author of the book, **Inside American Education: The Decline, The Deception, The Dogmas,** said, *"If every parent in America knew what was really going on in the public schools, there would be a revolution."*

Here are some examples of what our schools deal with daily:

- In 2011, the number of babies born to teens in the US was 329,797.[1] According to the National Center for Education Statistics,

- In 2011, data from the National Crime Victimization Survey showed that more victimizations were committed against students ages 12–18 at school than away from school. This pattern has been consistent since 2001. In

2011, students ages 12–19 experienced 1,246,000 nonfatal victimizations (theft and violent crime) at school, compared to 965,200 nonfatal victimizations away from school. These figures represent total crime victimization rates of 49 crimes per 1,000 students at school and 38 victimizations per 1,000 students away from school."[2]

- According to a recent bulletin released by the Office of Juvenile Justice and Delinquency Prevention, 23 percent of students aged 12 through 18 reported that street gangs had been present at their school during the previous 6 months. Almost half (46%) of students in public schools reported a street gang presence, with 21 percent of students in suburban schools and 15 percent in rural schools reported the presence of street gangs. [3]

- The International Planned Parenthood Federation (IPPF) at the UN is calling for a society that allows a child from birth on to express his/her sexuality. If this were the case, pedophilia and child pornography would no longer be a crime.

- At DeWitt Clinton High School in the Bronx, agents keep an overstuffed locker filled with confiscated weapons in the dean's office," one school safety agent stated in a lawsuit filed last year. Also mentioned was the fact that "Gangs and violence [are] rampant in public schools throughout the city [New York].[4]

- In July 2013, the California state legislature passed what has been dubbed as "the bathroom law" where a child K–12 can choose his/her own gender, then be allowed to use the bathroom of the chosen gender as well as the sports team he/she chooses.[5]

- Since 1992, there have been 387 separate instances of school shootings in the US that resulted in 492 students and school staff deaths.[6]

- The National Department of Education's *Green Agenda* was stated by Secretary of Education Arne Duncan during a September 2010 Summit: Citizenship and Pathways for a Green Economy. Duncan said, "Preparing our children to be good environmental citizens is some of the most important work any of us can do."[7]

- In 2009, the Los Angeles Unified School District misappropriated $158 million from its cafeteria fund. The LAUSD held a press conference to make an appeal for more funds to feed the children.[8]

- Over the past decade the Los Angeles Unified School district (LAUSD) spent $3.5 million trying to fire seven of the district's 33,000 teachers for poor classroom performance—only four were fired after lengthy legal struggles.[9]

- On August 5, 2013, AOL ran an article on its news briefs, "Student-Teacher Sex Scandal" featuring 43 cases where female teachers were charged with statutory rape. And that is only the tip of the iceberg.

- The National Institute of Literacy recent study stated that 4% of all adults in the US are illiterate, 14% of the adults in this country can't read. The number of adults who can't read above a fifth grade level is 21%. A whopping 19% of our high school graduates walk away from high school unable to read.[10]

- In our prisons, 63% of the inmates can't read at a 5th grade level.[11]

- US students scored 37th (overall) in International Rankings on the Program for International Student Assessment (PISA) tests. PISA is a global achievement exam given to fifteen-year-olds.[12]

- The United States spends $12,743 per year per student, more than any other nation in the world.[13]

- The NEA is the supplier of most Environmental Curricula for our public schools.

- About 17 percent of American high school students are drinking, smoking or using drugs during the school day, according to a new study by the National Center on Addiction and Substance Abuse.[14]

- In the United States, it is estimated 1.2 million students annually drop out of high school. High school graduation rates in the United States rank 22nd in the world.[15]

- Eight percent of teenagers between the ages of 16 and 19 are not enrolled in school or employed (full or part-time). They are referred to as Idle Teens or Disconnected Youth.[16]

- Nearly one in five high school age boys in the United States and 11 percent of school-age children over all have received a medical diagnosis of attention deficit hyperactivity disorder (ADHD), according to new data from the federal Centers for Disease Control and Prevention.[17]

- In the US," according to a teen organization called TeenHelp.com, "it's estimated that one in every 200 girls between 13 and 19 years old, or one-half of one percent, cut themselves regularly. Those who cut comprise about 70 percent of teen girls who self injure. Two of the most alarming facts about teen cutting are these: the number of cases is on the rise, and without treatment, many who begin cutting themselves as teens will continue the behavior well into their adult years.[18]

- According to the Centers for Disease Control and Prevention, 47.4 percent of high school students surveyed have had sexual intercourse. Of that number, 33.7 percent had had sexual intercourse during the previous 3 months. Those who had had sex with four or more people during their life was 15.3 percent.[19]

- In many schools, 75 percent of the students are functioning at two or more grade levels below where they currently are placed.[20]

- Added to the above dismal statistics, the church is losing the next generation.

- Ninety percent of Christians send their children to government sponsored public schools.[21]

- Over sixty percent of the children raised in Christian homes and who grow up going to church, will leave the church as they become young adults.[22]

Could we have reached the law of diminishing returns in our educational system? If so what is behind the fact that children in our schools are more at risk than ever before? Why are they not learning? As the apostle Paul states in 2 Timothy 3:7, we are "always learning but never able to acknowledge the truth." He goes on to say, "Just as Jannes and Jambres opposed Moses, so also these men oppose the truth—men of depraved minds, who, as far as the faith is concerned, are rejected" (v. 8).

For the amount of money we invest in education, we should have the best schools in the world. Is the answer to give more money to education? At what point do we realize that the great experiment implemented by key godless educators like Horace Mann, known as the father of public education, and John Dewey, known as the father of modern education, has failed? We just saw that the US spends $12,743 per year on each public school student, according to the US Department of Education. That number far exceeds the per student cost in any other country in the world, even those countries that outperform us on international exams like the PISA (Program for International Student Assessment).

In response to the PISA 2013 dismal results, where our 15 year olds scored thirty-fourth in math among other developed nations, Arne Duncan (head of the US Department of Education) said:

"The big picture of US performance on the 2012 PISA is straightforward and stark. It is the picture of educational stagnation.... The brutal truth, that urgent reality, must serve as a wakeup call against educational complacency and low expectations.[23] ...We must invest in early education, raise academic standards, make college affordable, and do more to recruit and retain top-notch educators."[24]

Duncan's answer is to spend more money, which is a socialistic view. He also suggests the government should take our children at an even earlier age away from their parents and put them in public schools, give more money to colleges and pay teachers higher salaries. No, Mr. Duncan, what we need is a moral and spiritual revival in our schools, along with a return to the biblical teachings that proved effective for the earliest settlers who came to this country in search of religious and individual freedom. With the current thought by prominent educators like Duncan, education does not look like it will get better. We need a different path altogether, one that will manifest as we bind the strongman over education and deal with root causes.

The church has, for the most part, abandoned our nation's schools, due in part to the secularization of our education, which has excluded the church and God from participating in everything from curriculum writing to moral teaching. Having few options, many believers pull their children out of public schools for homeschooling; others place their children in Christian schools.

Christians have not known how to combat the tide of evil perpetrated upon them by the American educational system. On the other hand, the schools are floundering and have no clue how to regain their footing. To say things are bad is a gross understatement. But if faith-filled believers will take the challenge to pray for American education, not back down, and stick with a prayer plan, they will win.

3 What is the Mountain of Education?

The Seven Mountain Theory was first proposed around 1975 by four prominent ministers: Bill Bright, founder of Campus Crusade; Loren Cunningham, founder of Youth With A Mission; Francis Schaeffer, founder of L'Abri; and Pat Robertson, founder of Christian Broadcasting Network. These ministers concluded that if Christians were to change a society they would have to affect seven areas or mountains of influence. While other ministers also had a similar understanding of how to change culture, the Seven Mountain discovery became known as the brainchild of Bright and Cunningham.

Those seven mountains are business, arts, religion, family, media, education and government. Each mountain is comprised of all the people who make up that cultural force. However, not everyone in that mountain has the same amount of influence. Those who have positions of influence are at the top of the mountain, and the top is comprised of 3–5 percent of the total number of people in the mountain. Those influencers are the ones who make policy decisions that determine the ethical behavior of the rest of the mountain.

So how do we influence the top of the mountain? We need to look at the cultural force of education to find out.

The **Mountain of Education** is one of the seven mountains of influence in the culture of our nation. It consists of the sum of every element from early learning centers to universities that comprise our educational system. Included in this mountain are curriculum writers, students, teachers, support staff, school board members, educational service staff, parents, National Board of Education, every state board of education, professional organizations like the NEA and other labor unions that represent school staff, administrators, extracurricular activities and other programs that make any effort to discipline the minds and character of the American people through study or instruction.

Efforts to influence the educational system in America can be overwhelming because of the sheer enormity of all that is involved. But if three key elements come together, they will help us to look at our educational system in the realm of the Spirit: 1) seeing education as a cultural mountain in our nation; 2) spiritually mapping the educational system; 3) learning to contend with the ancient thrones of iniquity over our educational system. Then, and only then, will we see where it can be affected and turned around to save our children and our country. We've been talking about the first key element; let's continue on and look more in depth at the other two.

4 Spiritual Mapping

Spiritual Mapping combines data collection, historical research and spiritual revelation that pertain to a particular geographical region, family, or profession. The combination of knowledge enables one to identify the strategies and methods of the spiritual forces of darkness that are in the current state of manifestation in that region, family or profession. In my case, I wanted to know why the American educational system was in such a state of disarray and why it seemly couldn't change. The ultimate goal in my mapping exercise was the development of a prayer strategy that would address the spiritual root causes that allowed darkness and destruction to continually reign over our schools and our children.

One prime example of effective spiritual mapping occurred in Oklahoma City after the 1995 bombing of the Murrah Building where 168 people were killed and 680 people were injured. The apostolic and prophetic leaders in Oklahoma spiritually mapped the Oklahoma City area and unveiled past sins, such as: broken covenants with the Native Americans; massacres of Native Americans; the Land Run, which stole land from the Native Americans; and the 1921 Tulsa Race

Riot, which left an untold number of African-Americans dead, many of their bodies thrown in the Arkansas River.

Because I'd spent most of my working life as a junior high and high school mathematics teacher, I knew that the Mountain of Education would be my focus. Another factor that made me interested in education was that seven years prior to my exposure to the Seven Mountain Strategy, C. Peter Wagner (a Christian author, missionary, and teacher) had conducted a retreat in Colorado Springs, Colorado for professionals from different occupations to spiritually map their respective professions.

Spiritual mapping is usually done on geographical regions, so this was a new concept and, to my knowledge, was the first time that spiritual mapping had been done on professions. Wagner had worked closely with George Otis Jr., director of The Sentinel Group, an organization that was actively involved in the transformation of geographic regions. Wagner wanted to take spiritual mapping to a new level, asking doctors, teachers, financial planners and other people to look at the history of their respective professions with spiritual eyes.

Otis defines *spiritual mapping* as a tool that allows believers to investigate the spiritual dynamics of their communities. It is the process of data acquisition for pastors, intercessors, worshipers and evangelists to analyze, strategize and process their evangelistic efforts.

My dear friends Drs. Mark and Betsy Neuenschwander headed up the meetings which took place in Colorado Springs, Colorado. Approximately thirty people from different professions came together to determine how our profession had arrived at its present state, good or bad. Then we were to devise a comprehensive prayer plan that would enable a novice to pick up our outline and pray effectively for any one of the professions. We were in a war room directing a war in the realm of the Spirit by putting together a spiritual warfare plan that any prayer warrior could use.

As an educator, I knew the educational system in the United States had changed, and not for the better. I'd watched it fail before my eyes. When I was in school, the problems in a classroom were simple—gum chewing, tardiness and occasionally truancy. In the classroom twenty years later, I now dealt with drugs, alcohol, low test scores, disrespect and outright rebellion. I delved back into history to find where the United States educational system had taken turns that led us down the path to a totally different school environment than our parents and grandparents had experienced. It soon became clear what had happened.

5 Praying Through History

It were as though a mastermind had led us to the point of destruction. That evil mastermind turned out to be none other than Baal, the false god of the Old Testament. The Greeks had perpetuated worship to Baal, as had the Romans. Later, the salons[25] of France gave new life to humanism, which is a form of Baal worship. Many of our country's founding fathers were influenced by France's "enlightenment" and brought those ideas to America. .

The goal of the Colorado Springs group of professionals was to merge the Mountain of Influence teaching with spiritual mapping, then identify the ancient thrones of iniquity and major spiritual influences in our educational system. At that point, we could deal with them in prayer. It's a simple strategy, yet profound.

Perhaps because the educational system is huge, it looks overwhelming to take on as a prayer effort. For the most part, prayer efforts for education have been to pray for some aspect of the system that influences us directly—for instance, a mother might pray for the school and teachers where her children attend classes. But intercession for the whole of education is seldom done and most likely is a result of intercessors not being summoned and given the tools to know how to pray for the educational system as a whole.

The system is in dire need of revision, revival, and reformation, but how to pray for those changes often eludes us as intercessors. The result has been that the system has run rampant with limited moral checks and balances. As a consequence, our nation has reaped the negative benefits of godless education administered by those who wish to educate a person's mind to the exclusion of the spirit.

Education has to be reclaimed as a part of reformation in America. How is that to be accomplished? Many of us who are over the age of fifty have seen the American educational system make a steady downturn. Can we take it back? Can we make a difference? Can our educational system be turned around? I believe it can. If we will listen to the leadership God has placed in authority over this mountain, things will change. God is unfolding His strategy on how to pray and change education, which will ultimately result in a change in our country.

Jesus said, **"How can anyone enter a strong man's house and carry off his possessions unless he first ties up the strong man? Then he can rob his house"** (Matthew 12:29). In America's beginnings we had a godly educational system based on godly principles. Over time godless decisions were made and evil entered in, slowly at first, but once a foothold was gained the floodgates of evil were opened and our educational system became so corrupt that many doubt if it can be redeemed at all. As intercessors, we must leave the results of our prayers to God. It may be that He will see fit to raise up another educational system parallel to the one in existence today. Who knows how He will answer our prayers?

Reclaiming our educational system won't be molding a school system in the image of all Christian schools. Nor will it be to bring about a system like we enjoyed 60 years ago. It is about advancing the Kingdom of God. How do we go about advancing the Kingdom of God in education? Sounds like a lofty spiritual goal, but God does give specific instructions as to how we are to establish His Kingdom on this earth. With over 100,000 (as per the US Department of Education web site) public schools in this country, this is a huge task. However, if we have a plan, we can change the system.

Our assignment is to take back education in America. We will outline a strategy, set forth a plan and then go before the Courts of Heaven and present our case.

6 Where Does Change Start?

In October 1944, Viktor Frankl, a young Austrian neurologist and psychiatrist, was transported to Auschwitz, a Nazi concentration camp located in Poland. His young wife, Tilly, was transported to a different camp. He never saw her again. In all, Frankl survived three years under Nazi control in ghettos and camps. When he arrived at Auschwitz, he had hidden a copy of the manuscript of his new work in his jacket with the hope that the Nazis would allow him to keep it. The precious writings were destroyed and Frankl had to start over with a new manuscript. His work, *Man's Search for Meaning*, is now considered a classic as Frankl shares insights into people's actions when their situation looks hopeless.

"When we are no longer able to change a situation...we are challenged to change ourselves," Frankl said.[26] He realized the importance of a person starting with an inner journey of change that would ultimately change the world.

Any change in a culture starts right where you are. One misconception is that change always starts at the top level of administration. Whatever the culture, change can start top down or bottom up. In the education culture, either way it starts it will

25

eventually link the concerned parent with the head of the Department of Education. The two will connect because reformation of a culture engages people at every strata of society. Of utmost importance is knowing that change starts with each person reading this book.

Everyone can pray and that's why this book was written—to help guide you to pray for education in America. If we have the correct prayer strategy and we work together in agreement, education in America will change. It will not have a choice. First, intercessors must believe that it is possible.

When the influential English Parliamentarian William Wilberforce altered the course of England, it is said that the change was made when every fisherman's wife realized that God loved her and she could pray and get her prayers answered! In other words, the very common person on the streets of England could experience a relationship with God. Although Wilberforce is credited with changing England by ridding the country of the horrible slave trade and creating a revival of morals in the country, he could not have accomplished such great feats of revival without the undergirding of the common folk of the land.

The situation we face in our nation is not unlike what the prophet Ezekiel faced in Israel hundreds of years earlier. In Ezekiel 22, the Bible lists Jerusalem's sins. Ezekiel called it a "city of bloodshed," full of "detestable practices" (v. 2). They worshiped idols, committed shameful sexual acts; they devoured people, shed innocent blood, committed extortion, robbery, oppressed the poor, and mistreated the alien. Their sins were great, yet the Lord said, "I looked for a man among them who would build up the wall and stand before me in the gap on behalf of the land so I would not have to destroy it, but I found none" (v. 30).

God is looking for men and women to stand in the gap before Him and the sins of the people so that He can once again bless the land. God is constantly searching for those who, although they acknowledge how far our educational system has drifted from its

Godly heritage, are willing to take a stand before God in prayer on behalf of our children and our nation.

The first goal in transforming our educational system is to identify the root causes of why our system became corrupt. The second goal is to engage people to pray strategic, effective prayers for education in America. If, in an answer to those prayers, God allows people to be positioned in political offices, appointments and jobs in education, that would be wonderful. God desires to have Godly people as gatekeepers in the educational field. The positioning of key people in education will occur as effective prayers are prayed. Yet foremost there must be a solid, workable prayer strategy.

7 Why Is Education Being Attacked?

Albert Einstein, considered by many to be the most influential physicist in the twentieth century, once said, "We cannot solve our problems with the same thinking we used when we created them." Education is in the failed state it is today because a faulty system of thinking was put in place at distinct points in its history. One would think that if those in administrative authority knew that what they did wasn't working, they would change their thinking immediately. But change doesn't happen when faulty thinking is a spiritual stronghold that resists it.

Many of us on the outside of the system think, *Why? What's the purpose for the self-destructive actions our government* [mainly the judicial system] *is promoting?* A close observation reveals that it is all about God, and not just any god, but the God of Abraham, Isaac, Jacob and Jesus. There is an intense desire by some secularists to do away with all vestiges of the God who created the universe and gave man free will to develop his talents, earn a living by working at a profession of his own choosing, and worship God according to the dictates of his own conscience.

What is the real reason that prayer, Bible reading, and the Ten Commandments were taken out of schools? The reason was to get rid of the God of the Christians. It's a fact—students are not free to mention God in commencement speeches, at sporting events, in art fairs, or any other public school arena. Christmas holidays are now winter holidays. The mere mention of God in schools seems to strike fear in the hearts of many who believe that man is god.

It is the God the Christians serve who is the target. Since a belief in God enables people to enjoy liberty by resisting the tyranny of socialism, it makes sense that those who would like to impose socialism or communism on the United States would first attack God.

Wilberforce wrote two hundred-plus years ago, "It is a truth attested by the history of all ages and countries…that the religion and morality of a country, especially of every free community, are inseparably connected with its preservation and welfare… It has been even expressly laid down, that people grossly corrupt are incapable of liberty."[27]

Sadly, government and our educational system run parallel to each other. When one looks at the condition of the schools, there is a direct reflection on the condition of our government. They are intertwined. Healing of the school system will result in healing our government, and Socialists do not want the government healed. As long as those who are anti-God control our schools they will be able to lead our government down the path to socialism and eventually communism. Vladimir Lenin, the man who led the Bolshevik Revolution in 1917 said, "Give me four years to teach the children and the seed I have sown will never be uprooted."

American freedoms are on the line and there is a battle going on for the people of America that is being fought in our classrooms. The spiritual heritage of our nation is being destroyed in the clash of two world views—socialism versus free markets. The reformation of America's schools will facilitate the reformation of our country.

8 Why Can't the System Change?

I recently asked a teacher, "Why don't you think the educational system can change?" I valued her opinion and wanted to hear what she had to say.

"I don't really know," she replied. "I have some ideas, but I'm not sure what's keeping things stuck. I do know that it's bad and really needs change. The kids suffer and the teachers are discouraged. It's hard to imagine why the administration makes the decisions they make. I wonder what in the world they are thinking? Maybe that's the problem—they aren't thinking."

To try to figure out what other people are thinking is a dangerous pastime. It's far better to look beyond the obvious decision for the spiritual roots of what is going on. A prime example happened one year when my intercessory prayer group participated in The Call, a massive prayer meeting held in Washington, DC. Approximately 100,000 people from all over America gathered on the area located between the Capital Building and the Washington Monument called The Mall, to repent for the sins of our nation and then pray for restoration. One of the speakers was a lady who had had multiple abortions. She related how the first abortion was a benchmark in her

31

life that drastically altered her future. Her life had spun out of control. She was miserable, got into trouble with the law, started using drugs, prostituting herself, lying compulsively, and eventually had her children taken away by the Department of Human Services.

Despite her desperation for normalcy, she couldn't keep a job or stay in a meaningful relationship so jobs and partners came and went in rapid succession. Yet, she couldn't connect the dots to the one action that had caused such misery in her life. The abortion was legal and therefore not wrong, so what was going on? She was unable to get a grip on her life until she realized that abortion was a sin and at the root of her problems. She repented and afterwards the restlessness left and she was able to keep a job. From there she pulled her life back together.

Several other women shared similar stories. They didn't cry, ask for sympathy or otherwise pull on the emotions of the audience. They simply shared the facts. I thought of the women whom I knew who'd had abortions. Many of them were like those women, their lives out of control and they had no clue why.

The same is true of our educational system. In the past, some very wrong and godless decisions were made and no repentance has ever been done for those decisions. Our education system is out of control and no one knows why or what to do about it. We don't know how to rein it back to some form that makes sense and enables our system to produce well-educated children. The lives of innocent children are at stake. We have set ourselves on a self-destructive course and no one seems to know how to redirect America's education.

What if the simple act of identifying the spirit of control over our educational system, repenting and renouncing that spirit could turn things around? What if we could look at our history and realize where those decisions were made that turned us against a loving God? What if we could change the fallout from those decisions with repentance and prayer? Wouldn't it be worth any effort needed to redeem the future of our children and our nation?

Change will require dedicated intercessors committed to long-term efforts. The ancient thrones of iniquity must be identified and properly disengaged from the educational system, and a prayer strategy developed and implemented. It's a doable plan that will work.

9 Identifying the Strongman

On Monday, October 21, 2013, a 12-year-old middle school student in the small town of Sparks, Nevada, took a gun to school and opened fire, killing one teacher and injuring two students before turning the gun on himself. Tuesday, October 22, 2013, in Massachusetts, a fourteen-year-old student attacked his 24-year-old mathematics teacher with a box-blade cutter, killing her. He disposed of her body in a wooded area near the school.

On October 24, 2013, an eleven year-old boy at Frontier Middle School located in Vancouver, Washington was arrested for bringing a gun and 400 rounds of ammunition to school. He allegedly was intending to shoot a classmate who bullied his friend and called him gay.

Events like these are everyday occurrences in our schools. Who is really to blame? Certainly the children are responsible for their actions, but what spiritual authority rules over the educational system that allows the atrocities that we have seen in our schools over the past fifty plus years?

Public schools run a continual ticker tape of incidences of violence that takes place on a regular basis in the classrooms. Sad to say, the crimes that make the headlines are usually gun/death related, and the thousands upon thousands of assaults on teachers, assaults by teachers, thefts, incidents of vandalism, rapes by teachers, rapes of teachers, rapes of students by students, and so on are never revealed to the general public.

We already know that the situation is dire, but we secretly hope that it isn't as bad as we think. It would be over simplistic to attribute all the instances of violence to bad teachers, guns, emotional problems in students, ADHD, emotional disturbances, overworked teachers, crowded classrooms, drugs or the many other issues our public schools face. To deal with these issues are to deal with symptoms. As intercessors, we need to dig deeper into what is happening and truly deal with the spiritual darkness that is the root cause of chaos in our schools.

At the memorial service for the dead 45 year-old mathematics teacher in Sparks, Nevada, Julia Rubin, a community leader from Reno's Temple Sinai said, "We pray after we have mourned and comforted each other we can take steps to address the root cause of violence and gun use by children throughout our country."[28] Yes, Rubin has the correct prayer—that we address the root cause of violence and gun use by children.

This book deals with remedies for overthrowing the powers of darkness and principalities and for breaking curses over our educational system. (Ephesians 6:12 NKJV.) This is a book of war— war in the realm of the spirit so those who choose to intercede on behalf of our nation and our children will be able to push back the forces of darkness, reveal the roots that have held us in bondage, and allow our children to be set free. Then the institution of education will be set free and our children will be educated not only in knowledge but in Godly spiritual principles.

10 Ancient Thrones of Iniquity

Going back to the roots of idol worship in the Old Testament we find Baal as the primary idol. According to *Vine's Dictionary*, Baal can denote any deity other than the one true God of Israel, Creator of heaven and earth. (See Isaiah 65:16 NIV; 1 Corinthians 8:6 KJV.) Baal was worshiped by the Canaanites, the people Israel was instructed to destroy once they entered the promised land.[29]

Throughout their history the Israelites lived in a vicious cycle of worshiping Baal and then turning back to God after their idol worship had sent them into darkness and despair. *Baal* is also another name for "lord" or "master."[30] He has a masculine and a feminine persona. John Benefiel points out in his book ***Binding the Strongman Over America*** that Baal while translated "lord" also means "possessor" or "owner."[31]

Baal was worshiped as the god of fertility by the Canaanites. They believed he gave fertility to the womb and rain to the earth. *Baal worship* is putting faith and trust in something that is made by man's hands. Baal was man's attempt to create a deity apart from the one true God. This is exactly the point to which we have arrived in our educational system.

Another idol that surfaces time and again when dealing with the destruction of children is the false god of Molech. Baal and Molech are two prominent idols worshiped in the Old Testament. The prophet Jeremiah speaks of Baal being the one dominate of the two.

> **They set up their abominable idols in the house that bears my Name and defiled it. They built high places for Baal in the Valley of Ben Hinnom to sacrifice their sons and daughters to Molech, though I never commanded, nor did it enter my mind that they should do such a detestable thing to make Judah sin.**
>
> **Jeremiah 32:34,35** NIV

First the people worshiped Baal and then they gave their children as a sacrifice to the god Molech. The earliest mention of Molech in the Bible is in Leviticus 18:21, which says, "Thou shalt not let any of thy seed pass through the fire to Molech, neither shalt thou profane the name of thy God: I am the Lord" (KJV).

In our schools today, we have followed the pattern of worshiping Baal. We did this by taking any mention of the one true God out of the curriculum, eliminating prayer and Bible reading from our schools, purging any reference to God from the classrooms, and by esteeming any religion on equal footing with Christianity. This worship of Baal has allowed the worship of Molech to enter. Now we face the destruction of our children by abortions and killings, not only in their bodies but also their minds and spirits.

Baal is often pictured as a man on a bull. Molech is depicted as a bull with hands lifted up to the heavens and whose breast has seven chambers to hold sacrifices. The first chamber held flour, the second two turtle doves, the third a ewe, the fourth a ram, the fifth a calf, the sixth an ox, and the seventh a living child. During a ceremony, a fire would be set in the bottom chamber and as the heat and flames leapt upwards in intensity the seven chambers that held the sacrifices would all be consumed.

Does that same concept of creating something to worship apart from the one true and living God still exist today? Absolutely! Today our educational system promotes the search for wisdom and intellectual knowledge apart from God. Anytime man attempts to educate the mind and not the spirit, the result is idol worship and the consequences are the same as what the Israelites faced each time they strayed from serving God—darkness and despair.

Molech is always associated with killing children. The forces of evil are continually searching for ways to abort future generations. Nowhere in our society are children being killed more than through abortion, suicide, drugs, and school shootings. Not only are they physically in danger, their futures are being sacrificed through unproven humanistic teaching practices. They are being taught that abortion is okay, promiscuousness is not a sin, sexual perversion is acceptable, and immorality is relative.

11 Where Did It Start?

Killing future generations is a design of the enemy and certainly not a new problem. While we look at our abortion statistics since 1962, we might think that the problem started then. After all, we have, in this country alone, aborted over 54,000,000 babies since abortion became legal.[32] Now through US nonprofits and the UN, we export the practice of abortion to other countries. We do it so that a woman may have choices—she may choose between having a family and a career.

Whenever God is left out of any institution the result is destruction. We have abandoned serving the one true God and the consequences are not good. In Deuteronomy 28:25, one of the curses listed for Israel if they turned from serving God was that they would be defeated by their enemies. The good news is that if we repent, He will forgive and redeem our school system and America.

The false gods of Baal and Molech have held spiritual darkness in place over our children and allowed destruction to flow from one generation to another. Intercessors must deal with the spiritual strongman over our entire educational system. The root of humanism is rooted in Baal worship. We have been unable to combat the tide of humanist influence that has not only prevailed in American schools, but has flourished. Why has this happened? It is because we have continued to allow the root to grow.

Evil is like a buried root that continues to produce new growth. As long as the root of the sin lives, evil vines will continue to grow from that root. As we divorce ourselves from Baal and Molech, we will be able to release the Spirit of God into the atmosphere through repentance, prophetic prayers, proclamations, and other prophetic means.

Only then will curses over our nation, our children, and our families be broken. Symptoms of a strong anti-God spirit in our schools include out-of-control classrooms, illiterate high school graduates and humanism being taught with the most obvious result being the removal of prayer and Bible reading from public schools. All of these are very real problems in our schools, but are also symptoms of a central power behind it all.

John Benefiel's book *Binding the Strongman Over America* is a must read for anyone dealing with spiritual wickedness over regions and areas in the United States. God released a prophetic word recently at a national conference that unveiled Baal as the strongman over America. God said we must divorce ourselves from Baal and remarry the Lord Jesus. (See Hosea 2:19–20 NKJV.) One of the major accomplishments the Heartland Apostolic Prayer Network (HAPN) happened as Dr. Benefiel commissioned teams to go to every abortion clinic in the United States to pray—and pray they did! As of this writing 12 states have passed legislation that place restrictions on abortions, especially late term abortions.

States that HAPN never suspected as leaders in the anti-abortion movement, like Nebraska, have enacted legislation to stop late-term abortions. Headway was made in surprising ways, which is how God does something—we pray and allow Him to move. We don't tell Him how to answer.

12 A Different Way to Fight

My first meeting with Roberta Hromas was in 2000. I had taken a group from Tulsa, OK, to Washington, D.C. to pray for our nation. My group stayed at the prayer house Roberta owns. It is located directly across the street from the Israeli Embassy. Roberta happened to be in Washington, D.C. at the same time. One of the nights we were there, Roberta met with our group and we learned that her father was Charles Parham who is considered by many to be the Father of the modern day Pentecostal movement. Roberta has followed in her father's footsteps as a woman of prayer and action. So when Roberta shared one of the ways God led her in spiritual warfare, I listened intently.

Roberta felt impressed by the Holy Spirit to identify the twenty most evil places on the earth where humans had engaged in pagan idol worship. Some of the locations were sites where human sacrifices had been made. At each location she was to sing praises to God, and lift up the Name of Jesus. Roberta was in her 60s when she was given this assignment, which entailed her traveling to some of the most remote and environmentally hostile places on earth.

One site in China was so remote that the only access was by boat. So she hired boatmen to guide her down the river to the place where human sacrifices had been made. It took her over ten years to complete her assignment, but she faithfully fulfilled the commitment. When asked if she suffered backlash from going to these evil places, she replied, "Absolutely not. I serve the most powerful God on earth and He protected me." Since our assignment is to bind the strongman over American education, it is well to remember Roberta's affirmation that God will protect us.

Roberta didn't travel to the evil places to come against the powers of darkness or attack demons in the natural. She went to lift up high praises to the one true God. That is exactly what we will do with the forces of evil in education. We will pray positive prayers; we will divorce Baal and make positive declarations over every educational venue and entity. Where there is darkness we will bring light! Where there is hopelessness we will bring hope. Our job is to magnify God and bring His Kingdom to this earth.

When those who believe in Jesus go to war, we fight in different ways than those fighting a political war. The apostle Paul wrote,

For though we live in the world, we do not wage war as the world does. The weapons we fight with are not the weapons of the world. On the contrary, they have divine power to demolish strongholds. We demolish arguments and every pretension that sets itself up against the knowledge of God, and we take down every thought to make it obedient to Christ. 2 Corinthians 10:3–5

There is no better place to test our spiritual mettle than in prayer for the educational system in this country. For too long it has embodied a set of ideals that provide arguments and give pretensions that are contrary to God. They are the same humanist ideals that Voltaire and Rousseau (French Enlightenment writers and philosophers) penned in the eighteenth century, which emphasize learning and mind development as the equivalent of the highest spiritual experience. These teachings exalt man as a god unto himself.

Prayer to Bind the Spirit of Baal

Father, In the Name of Jesus I come to you. I recognize that the spirit of Baal has been unleashed in our schools and consequently on the children of this nation. I come to You in the Name of Jesus, that Name which is above every name—including the name of Baal. You have seated Jesus at Your right hand in the heavenly realms, far above all rule and authority, power and dominion, and every title that can be given, not only in the present age but also in the one to come (Ephesians 1:20–21). I pray that the Name of Jesus will be exalted above the name of Baal in every educational institution in America.

We are like Elijah who told King Ahab, "I have not made trouble for Israel... But you and your father's family have. You have abandoned the LORD'S commands and have followed the Baals"(1 Kings 18:18). Lord, may You reveal the roots of Baal worship in our schools and the problems that worship has caused. Reveal false prophets. I call on the Name of my God, the One who answers by fire (v. 24), to show Yourself strong to all who oppose You so that everyone will know that You turn people's hearts back to you (v. 37). May the Spirit of God come alive in every student in every school so that our children will cry, "You, O Lord, are God." Let all the people in education fall prostrate and cry, "You, O Lord, are God, and there is no other God beside You."

Just as Gideon tore down the altar of Baal his father had built (Judges 6:28–32), I, in the power of the Holy Spirit, tear down the altars to Baal in our educational system. Let the altar of the living God be exalted. We will praise the Name of the Lord as we lift up You and Your Son, Jesus, in every school in this nation. Amen. (This is an excellent place to declare the Baal Divorce Decree given in the Appendix.)

Prayer of Deliverance from the Spirit of Molech

Father, in the Name of Jesus I come to You and pray that the killing of our children will stop. The spirit of Molech will no longer operate in our nation and especially in our schools. I pray that our children will live and not die and declare the wondrous works of God. (Psalm 118:17.)

Your Word says that my battle is not against flesh and blood, but against powers and principalities and rulers in high places. (Ephesians 6:1,2.) So with that in mind, I bow my knee to the God and Father of my Lord Jesus Christ and I lift up the precious Name of Jesus, that Name that is above the name of Molech. I declare that Jesus is Lord over our school system. I speak life into the children of America. I worship You, Lord, and believe that Your power is greater than any other. We will give You praise for You have turned back our enemies and You have given us victory. I pray this in the Name of Jesus. Amen.

13 The Age of Reason

What has Greece got to do with the deep pagan roots of modern educational methods? The ancient Greeks instituted the educational philosophy called the *gymnasium* that became the foundation of our educational system. Aristotle, born 384 BC, was the first to write a comprehensive system of Western philosophy that included ethics, logic, science, politics, and metaphysics. As a student of Plato, Aristotle embraced Plato's idea of the gymnasium model of education where children were to be taken from their parents at an early age to be educated by the state.

He believed that if a child were separated from his parents, he could learn the habits and laws of the state. It is said that Friedrich Nietzsche, the German philosopher who greatly influenced Adolph Hitler, took nearly all of his political philosophy from Aristotle. John Dewey, a twentieth century American philosopher who greatly influenced educational and social reforms, was also influenced by Aristotle.

The Greek philosophers internalized the concept of idol worship. Baal appears in Greek culture as god in different forms, one of which is Columbia, a statue that adorns the top of our nation's capitol, another is the Statue of Liberty. But of great importance in education, the Greeks gave us the beginnings of the reasoning of the human mind apart from what they called the Muse or the inspiration of the spirit. The Greeks ushered in the age of human reason, or logic, that is associated with our thinking, cognition and intellect.

It was in Athens, the Greek city that was named for the goddess Athena, where Paul encountered a group of Epicurean and Stoic philosophers. The men met daily at a location called The Areopagus, which was also the name of the Athenian civil court. The Bible talks about Paul's encounter with them in Acts 17:21, where Paul says Areopagus was where "all the Athenians and the foreigners who lived there spent their time doing nothing but talking about and listening to the latest ideas."

After listening to Paul speak, the philosophers realized that they had no spiritual reference for what Paul was saying and openly admitted their lack of understanding. Was Paul advocating a foreign god because he was preaching the Good News of the Gospel? At this point, they invited Paul to come to a meeting of the Areopagus, in order for them to hear him expound on the subject of his God.

The Epicurean and Stoic philosophers were the humanists of their day. They enjoyed discussing ideas but had no concept of spiritual knowledge. *Epicurean* philosophy was based on materialism and denounced any divine intervention in the affairs of men. The Epicureans sought to live modestly and gain knowledge of how the world works in order to lead a life of tranquility, freedom from fear, and absence of bodily pain.

The *Stoics* believed that the pursuit of moral and intellectual perfection would not allow suffering. Both groups of philosophers, as well as all the Athenians, were involved in learning for the sake of acquiring knowledge. Daily they gathered at the Areopagus to discuss the latest ideas. Knowledge was the ultimate goal and learning was their god.

Paul started his speech to the Areopagus with reference to the "unknown god" to whom the Athenians had erected an altar. After his introduction, Paul immediately addressed the crowd about a personal God who made the world and everything in it. It's interesting to note that Paul didn't reprimand the Areopagian philosophers but rather added the dimension of a personal God to their knowledge. Although Athena is not mentioned in Paul's discourse, the elitist group of philosophers he addressed were well versed in knowledge about the goddess Athena, as her influence in the love of learning and the acquisition of knowledge was what brought them together.

In Greek mythology, Athena was the daughter of Zeus. The Greeks believed that she had sprung full grown from his head, wearing her helmet and armor. She was more warlike than the other goddesses and was almost always successful in her battles. As the goddess of wisdom and learning, the owl was her favorite bird because of its wise and solemn look. It is often pictured with Athena in the images that the Greeks made of her. Forever the learner, Athena was always looking for better ways of doing things. She taught men to use the plow and the rake and to yoke oxen so they could plow the soil more easily. Athena is the female counterpart of the male god Baal.

Aristotle's views provided fodder for intellectual discussions taking place in the meeting rooms and parlors, known as salons, of Europe during the Age of Enlightenment, originating about 1650 to the late 1700s. They gathered to discuss the newest ideas and to digest old ideas in the light of new scientific discoveries and humanistic revelations. The most famous salons were in France and fostered such philosophers as Voltaire and Rousseau.

In Germany, it was the famous philosopher Immanuel Kant who is considered a major contributor to modern philosophy. Thomas Paine was an English-American philosopher of the time who wrote a pamphlet that he distributed in the United States, the "Age of Reason." In it he stated, "I believe in one God, and no more, and I hope for happiness beyond this life.... All national institutions of churches, whether Jewish, Christian, or Turkish, appear to me no other than human inventions, set up to terrify and enslave mankind, and monopolize power and profit."[33]

Criticism of Christianity was not unusual. Any topic was fair game during The Age of Enlightenment

America's early founders like Thomas Jefferson, Benjamin Franklin, and George Washington were influenced by these new thinkers. Later, the founders of our educational system—Horace Mann and John Dewey—were also products of the Age of Enlightenment. Baal may change forms, but he never disappears.

14 Secular Education

York Preparatory Academy, a public charter school in Rock Hill, SC, allowed the students to help select the music for their Winter Program. According to one source, it "contained the songs 'Joy to the World' and 'O Come All Ye Faithful,' two traditional carols enjoyed during the Christmas season in churches, schools, communities and governments for generations." Suddenly the music was withdrawn from the program. Christmas carols were also banned from school programs in Wausau, Wisconsin, and New Jersey's Bordentown Regional School District.[34] In both cases, the school boards, reversed their decisions when they were provided with an explanation of the constitutional basis for allowing Christmas Carols in schools.

There is a growing trend to secularize our public schools and the process is done through the court system that scans education for religious breeches and files court cases to remove any mention of Christianity. The result of removing the Christians' mention of God from education does not give us secular education, but rather secular humanism. Education is a mind activity and throughout history, men and women, often of great intellect, who try to educate only the mind produce a religion that makes man his own god.

Those who came to this country in search of religious freedom educated not only the minds of our children but also their spirits. The Bible was used as a textbook and the teachers were, for the most part, Christians who imparted the Word of God as well as spiritual insights in the classrooms. We were truly blessed. Our children were taught to answer to God for acts of disobedience because they knew they were made by a Creator who expected good moral behavior. We were instructed in moral law.

The system of religious education has been under attack since its inception by ungodly men. They may have liked the product of our educational system, but they were not wise enough in the realm of the Spirit to know the source of what made us one of the most educated countries in the world. They thought education could be improved without God. It couldn't.

Ayn Rand, a Russian Jewish immigrant, escaped the horrors of the takeover of the Russian government in 1917 by Stalin and Lenin. Rand came to America and developed the philosophy of Objectivism, which praised the virtue of free markets (not a popular term in our public schools today). She stated, "The most profoundly revolutionary achievement of the United States of America was the subordination of society to moral law." She went on to say, "The United States was the first moral society in history."[35]

Rand may not have known that we were a moral society because our parents and our schools taught children to fear God, which then caused them to develop an internal moral code. However, she as a complete outsider to this country and to Christianity recognized what made us great. Things have changed dramatically, however, since this country embarked on a mission to totally exclude any references to the Christian God as schools began to address only knowledge. Our system went awry when we began to educate only the minds of our children.

Another attempt to secularize our education has come under the guise of **Separation of Church and State**. At least, that is the reason the US courts have handed down rulings that did things like take prayer out of schools, make it unlawful to teach anything but evolution, and prohibit Bible reading in schools. This has all happened in the last fifty years.

Separation of Church and State is a phrase that does not appear in our US Constitution. In spite of that, it has been used by our courts as though it were an integral part of our founding documents. Many of the framers of our Constitution were deists and wanted to make sure the abuses perpetrated by the Church of England would not happen in the United States. That is why they penned the First Amendment that prohibited the making of any law respecting the establishment of religion or impeding the free exercise of religion.

Our courts have also interpreted the establishment of religion clause to restrict the religious freedom that we have enjoyed in the country. Such loose interpretations have cost us many of the privileges we enjoyed as Christians and put us in a precarious situation because the rulings secularized our society, thereby giving way to secular humanism.

The sin of trying to circumvent God goes all the way back to the Garden of Eden when Eve and then Adam ate of the tree of the knowledge of good and evil. (Genesis 3.) From that time on, there was a battle in the realm of the Spirit. Every day since then man has had the choice to obey God or serve a false god. The predominant false god mentioned in the Bible is Baal. The spirit of Baal surfaces in a different form as it is internalized by the Greeks and then accepted by the Romans, who equate the reasoning of the mind as the equivalent of knowing God.

The challenge is to learn how to pray that this spirit of reasoning is dealt with so that it does not continue to influence our educational system in a negative way and consequently reap havoc on generation after generation of our children.

C. Peter Wagner, in his book *Warfare Prayer: How to Seek God's Power and Protection in the Battle to Build His Kingdom*, gives three levels of prayer:

1. Ground-level spiritual warfare

2. Occult-level spiritual warfare

3. Strategic-level spiritual warfare

Prayer strategies to reform American education belong in the highest level of warfare: Strategic-level spiritual warfare.[36]

In order to effectively engage in strategic-level prayer, an intercessor must have:

- Knowledge of being a born-again child of God.

- Belief in the power of the Name of Jesus.

- Belief in the work that Jesus did when He died on the cross and was raised again on the third day.

- Knowledge that the weapons of our warfare are not carnal but mighty through God to pull down strongholds.

- Knowledge of a legal right in the Courts of Heaven to reclaim our educational system.

- Knowledge in the power of praise and worship.

- Ability in the face of evil to make positive confessions and declarations.

- Submission to spiritual leadership.

There are many wonderful people who are praying for our schools. They do a terrific job and what they do is absolutely necessary. However, in order to have a transformation in our educational system, we need people of prayer who are willing to learn about the history of American education. Our nation's leaders made specific decisions to make our schools humanistic. If we are to see genuine change, it will require those who pray to have knowledge of those decisions and the spiritual impact they made for our nation. Prayer that creates a reformation is looking at the past, praying in the present, in order to impact the future.

15 What Is Required for Change?

John Davison Hunter, one of the leading Christian academics of this decade, in a 2002 Trinity Forum briefing, spoke on *"To Change the World."* Hunter stated, "Great ideas, in and of themselves, have very little value. It is only when those great ideas are connected to a network of influential people can they change the culture." Hunter cited Martin Luther as an example of a man who had a great idea—that salvation was a result of faith in Jesus and did not come through good works.

In 1517, Luther nailed his ninety-five theses to the door of the Castle Church of Wittenberg Germany, and set on course what we now call the Protestant Reformation. Luther's posting of his ninety-five points of contention with the Catholic Church might well have ended there had it not been for a network of people around him who carried his new idea about salvation to the corner of every village in Germany. Luther also had a network of people who hid him from danger. Others distributed literature, conducted meetings, and otherwise openly endorsed the Reformation.

It took a lot of what I call "influencers" to merge at one point in history to pave the way for Martin Luther's new revelation to impact millions. They carried a new prayer model that allowed them a personal relationship with Jesus.

If we look at the model Martin Luther used for the Protestant Reformation, the following elements were required:

- apostolic leadership with the idea for change;
- a network of influencers to carry those ideas forward;
- a prayer strategy;
- intercessors.

The same will be required for a true reformation in our educational system. A leader like Martin Luther will need to come to the forefront and many people will have to rally to take new ideas and reformation to its completion.

As intercessors, it is our responsibility to pray and believe for the right leader to come forth at the right time, with the right network. That's why I've included a prayer on which we could all agree for synergistic reformation in our educational system. We must include prayers for a viable network of apostolic leaders, influencers, prayer strategies, and intercessors. They may be educators, ministers, financiers, mothers, businessmen—people who will come from all walks of life to fulfill the mandate necessary to facilitate change in our nation.

Although I've mentioned William Wilberforce more than once, he is another great example of convergence as he led a movement to eradicate the slave trade and brought about a revival of morals in England. We see the intersection of key elements that made Wilberforce so effective. With his example, we have a pattern to devise a prayer strategy for the transformation of the educational system of America. Wilberforce was clearly an apostolic leader. He was charismatic, influential, and God placed him in the proper political position. Yet he would have never made such a mark in history if he hadn't had been flanked by a group of influencers known as the Clapham Circle.

The **Clapham Circle** was a like-minded group of reformers who came together every night in what Wilberforce termed as "The Better Hour" to dream of how England could be a better and more moral country. Wilberforce also had others who were committed to pray for a reformation in England and for the eradication of the slave trade. Today we can follow Wilberforce's example by creating prayer circles that will change our nation.

Prayer for Convergence

Father, I come to You in the Name of Jesus and I ask that as You changed the course of history in the birth of Your Son, Jesus, by calling Wise Men to come from the East with adoration and gifts of provision; shepherds to come from their fields; stars to appear in the heavens; angles to speak—change our schools by causing the events to converge for a reformation in America's educational system.

I pray for apostolic leaders to rise up who will be surrounded by like-minded men and women of influence. Give the correct prayer strategy so that intercessors will be able to pray in unity. Give us the prophetic declarations over our schools that need to be spoken in the realm of the Spirit.

I divorce the spirit of Baal and speak to this nation and declare that the strongman over our schools and every facet of our education is null and void. Our children will be allowed to serve You, the one true living God, who is above every name that is named in heaven and in earth. We believe You for signs and wonders in the heavens and on the earth as Your people come together to change education and bring America back to You. We pray this in the Name of Jesus. Amen.

16 Apostolic Leaders

Major-General Charles Orde Wingate (1903–1944) was one of the most interesting, innovative, and influential, aggravating, and outrageous British commanders of World War II. He was a deeply religious man who often used the Bible as a guide. In the English army, he was one of the forerunners of Special Operations Forces, who led his men on highly unorthodox and innovative missions. In 1936, he was assigned to Israel to put down the largest Palestinian uprising until the 1980s. The country was controlled by Arab bands that roamed through the streets at night, robbing, killing, stealing anyone and anything that came across their path.

Wingate persuaded the British and Zionist leaders to let him organize Special Night Squads. Dressed in casual khaki shorts and rubber soled shoes, they quietly walked single file in a zig-zag pattern throughout the city, surprising the notorious gangs. Because of their unusual military tactics Wingate said, "We were able to take back the night."[37] Later his men followed him when he led a small Gideon's force[38] against 300,000 Italian troops who were occupying East Africa.

Wingate is credited with turning the tide of the war that Japan waged against Burma in 1943 by the use of his Special Ops soldiers working behind enemy lines. They were a rag-tag bunch, looked down on by the organized military that attacked the enemy head-on. But Wingate's units of street savvy soldiers located strategically behind enemy lines were effective and powerful.

Here's what is unique about Wingate: his troops were small in number, their uniforms often looked like civilian dress, their tactics well thought out but unorthodox, yet they could secretly maneuver behind enemy lines and cause great damage to the enemy. Wingate said, "Given a population favorable to penetration, a thousand resolute and well-armed men can paralyze, for an indefinite period, the operations of a hundred thousand."[39]

Wingate was an apostolic leader who knew how to bring his troops together to make the greatest impact. As a leader, he was willing to go where no one else had gone before. He grasped an idea and persuaded others to embrace the concept and carry it through to completion.

The Church is in dire need of Wingate style of leadership and is in a state of disunity when there is a void in that area. We cannot change the culture without apostolic leaders. Just take a look at the way the Church is perceived in the political arena. We are fractured at every point. We lose elections that cost us moral ground. We cannot agree on one candidate to support. We are not recognized by our elected officials as a viable voting block; therefore, politicians pay little attention to Christians as a whole and our cultural concerns.

Even companies that support immoral practices don't listen to us. Recently there was an effort by some Christian groups to boycott Starbucks for the coffee company's stand on same sex marriage. Starbucks CEO, Howard Schultz, simply replied, "Let them buy their coffee and stocks someplace else." Shultz, also stated that if the investor didn't like the company's position, he was welcome to "sell [his] shares... and buy shares in another company. Thank you very much."[40] We as believers have lost our saltiness. We are no longer effective. While many Christians believe the days of leaders are over and each believer is a leader, history doesn't bear this out. Over the years people have risen or fallen on the basis of a leader who will call them to an action, either moral or immoral. That is why we need to pray for the right leaders to come forward to lead the reformation in American education.

William Wilberforce is such an excellent example of an apostolic leader that I have to mention something else regarding him. Many historians agree that had he not stopped the slave trade in England, which led to the ending of slavery in that country and then led England in a revival of morals, the country stood to cleanse itself through a bloody war, much like that of the French Revolution in the mid-1700s, considered to be the bloodiest revolution in history. America too had no Wilberforce and was not spared from a bloody civil war in the mid-1800s where over 600,000 fathers, sons, and brothers were killed on our own soil. There was no Wilberforce for France or for the United States.

Dr. Robert Clinton in his book *The Making of a Leader: Recognizing the Lessons and Stages of Leadership Development*[41] discusses the different stages a leader must go through to develop his character so that he can walk into a true leadership role. What Dr. Clinton calls *leadership convergence* is when a leader surfaces as an apostle of his time. That leader is ready to take on a leadership role that God has personally groomed him for throughout his life. That is when a William Wilberforce, a Winston Churchill, a Hudson Taylor, a Billy Graham, or a George Washington comes forward. *God, give us the apostolic leaders to lead the educational reformation!*

True leaders/apostles are brought forth as men and women who go through stages of spiritual growth until they are prepared for the ultimate task God has for them. Let's pray for those leaders whom God is grooming to stay true to their calling so they can step into position to lead the educational system out of impending doom into an age of establishing God's Kingdom on this earth and in this nation.

Let it begin with those who would bind the strongman over the **Mountain of Education**.

A leader will draw the right people into position. Someone has to step out and gather around him believers and networkers who will come into action. Leaders with followers are true apostles. Perhaps the most well-known true apostle—Paul—said,

> **"Now you are the body of Christ, and each one of you is a part of it. And in the church God has appointed first of all apostles, second prophets, third teachers, then workers of miracles, also those having gifts of healing, those able to help others, those with gifts of administration, and those speaking in different kinds of tongues."**
>
> **1 Corinthians 12:27,28**

At this point in history, our assignment as intercessors is to pray and believe God for all the necessary elements of cultural change to merge at just the right time. It will require a character-tested leader who can bring to the table a network of individuals who are willing to do whatever it takes to allow the Kingdom of God to be expressed through them.

How often do we hear believers talking about the return of Jesus? They want Jesus to come back and deliver them from this evil world. Too often they refuse to accept responsibility for their part in changing the world. They do little except wait, hoping to escape the calamity the news media says is imminent. All the while, Jesus is waiting on us to redeem the earth and to establish the Kingdom of God.

Prayer for Apostolic Leaders

Father, in the Name of Jesus, I come to You asking for the right apostolic leadership to come to the forefront of the educational reformation in the United States. I ask that this person be a man or woman of upstanding moral character who will faithfully execute the duties of the true calling of a reformer. Give him or her the support and the networkers needed to be successful. I ask this in the Name of Jesus. Amen.

17 Influencers

Wilberforce drew those around him who were the major influencers of his day. His biographer John Pollock in his book *William Wilberforce* said, "Wilberforce proved that a man can change his times, but that he cannot do it alone."[42] Wilberforce worked tirelessly but by his side were the major influencers of his day that met with him.

Something else Dr. Clinton wrote in his classic book *The Making of a Leader* is, "I have stated that a Godly leader is a person with God-given capacity and God-given responsibility to influence specific groups of God's people toward His purposes for the group."[43] People of godly influence in every facet of the educational system are needed. There are a multitude of schools, institutions, organizations, and service industries and we will need leaders in every one of them to make a change in education.

If we don't have Godly influencers, the ungodly will fill in the gaps. At the turn of the twentieth century, John Dewey, a humanist, came on the educational scene with a plan to educate a child to be socialistic, which Dewey believed would best prepare a child for the twenty-first century. Students in Dewey's time were mostly from

Christian families. He wanted to change the child's mindset and belief system from Christianity so that the Dewey-educated child would see himself as god and not be loyal to any one religion but would view each religion as equal.

At that time, the majority of students had a strong sense of individualism, which was a strong suit of our forefathers. Dewey wanted a child with a collective mindset, whose efforts would be for the good of mankind and not for the individual. In order to promote his ideas, Dewey surrounded himself with like-minded humanists. He presented scholarly papers—over seven-hundred in all—that promoted his supposedly new ideas.

While at the University of Chicago in the late 1800s, Dewey convinced the university to start laboratory schools teaching his new concepts. But by far his most strategic move was his connection with Harvard University and the National Education Association. At Harvard as well as other Ivy League colleges, Dewey found like-minded influencers who caught his vision of the trickle-down effect. That meant that they would present academic papers filled with new ideas to the elite of our nation who were able to attend prestigious universities. They then would take Dewey's ideas to less prestigious colleges as they accepted teaching positions at those schools. The ideas would filter down to the local schools as graduates of state colleges accepted positions in local schools.

Once he gained access to the influencers of the NEA, Dewey's ideas exploded exponentially on the educational scene. The association started adding not only educators, but also curriculum publishers and other school vendors.

It's the apostolic leader, in this case ,John Dewey, with the revolutionary idea with the right set of influencers who changed our nation. John Dewey certainly proved it was possible. American education has carried out his great experiment and it has given us inferior schools. Now it is up to us pray that his failed experiment will be reversed in American education.

Prayer for Influencers

Father, in the Name of Jesus, I come to You and ask for influencers to come to the forefront who will take the mantle of a new dimension of Spiritual Warfare for the educational system of the United States. I pray for those with moral integrity whose characters have been tested and proven genuine before You. Give them revelation knowledge. Give them meekness and humility as they work in unity with apostolic leadership. Let them blow the trumpet and declare a holy fast, call a sacred assembly, and gather the people. Let them unite the church to be instruments of change in this land so that our inheritance will not be an object of scorn, a byword among the nations. Bring us influencers after Your heart. Thank You for answering my prayer, in Jesus Name. Amen.

18 Apostolic Prayer Teams

In 1839, in the bowels of the ship *La Amistad*, were men taken from Sierra Leone to be sold as slaves in Cuba. One captive managed to pick the lock and loose the chains that bound his hands and feet. Once free, he unlocked the fetters from several of his companions. Together they killed all the crew except for the two owners. Taking control of the ship, they instructed the owners to navigate it back to West Africa. Six weeks later, *La Amistad* was found by a US military vessel off the coast of Long Island. It seems the two owners had steered the ship along the Atlantic coast instead of going toward the coast of Africa.

The Africans who had commandeered the ship were captured and imprisoned to await a court trial to determine who owned them or if they should be set free. At that point, the United States had banned the slave trade but not slavery, and was in a political quandary as to what to do with the men who, if they had landed in Cuba, would have been sold as slaves.

Abolitionists in the United States took up the cause of the men and asked the courts to grant the Africans freedom and safe passage back to their homeland of Sierra Leone. The case went to the Supreme Court, where many justices were from the south and threatened a civil war. John Quincy Adams gave a passionate speech in defense of the Africans that turned the court's decision. The Africans won and were given freedom and passage back to their homeland.

The 1997 movie *Amistad,* directed by Steven Spielberg, was based on the 1987 book by historian Howard Jones, ***Mutiny on the Amistad.*** In the movie, as the lawyers, justices, Africans, and witnesses filed in and out of court, they wove their way through a group of Christians who had positioned themselves on the lawn of the court house to intercede for a just outcome of the case. In a blatant display, the movie gave credit to the intercessors as God answered their prayer. As is the case, prayer has often turned the tide of historical events and will continue to be the catalyst for change in the future.

Prayer that alters the course of a nation is ***apostolic intercession.*** It is the prayer in which we must engage if we are to change the course of education in America. Prophetic intercessors will pray for our educational system with a spiritual and historical perspective. They know that it's crucial to cut off and divorce our association with those idolatrous roots, repent for wrong decisions, and pray on site at locations that have historical and spiritual significance to the whole educational system. This unique group is united for a common goal and works under an apostolic leadership to pray at a different spiritual level than those who engage in prayer for the daily operations for our schools and for the students. As apostolic intercessors, they are responsible for taking on the mantle of prayer for a large jurisdiction rather than one school or region.

Apostolic prayer teams pray on site. They go to specific locations and pray, make prophetic declarations, and enter into prophetic worship. They are the spearhead of a prayer initiative when reclaiming the land.

In this book, ten entry points have been identified and with each entry point there is a corresponding physical location that correlates with that entry point. Many people have already been on these sights to pray, and I hope others will do the same. If you can't pray at the specific location, you can go to a representative place near where you live. Neighborhood schools are abundant and provide a great place to pray. Other possibilities include educational buildings, service centers, state capitols, or school businesses.

Prayer Teams

Throughout my years praying at schools with prayer-walkers, I have always been astounded at who shows up to pray. Most of the time, I observed that those who prayed had no vested interest in the school and the children for whom they were praying. They were people— moms and dads, grandmothers (lots of these) and grandfathers—who wanted a better education for the children of America and were willing to come out on a cold, dark morning to pray on site at a local school. I learned long ago not to decide who would pray and who wouldn't but allow the Holy Spirit to bring those whom He would draw to pray for education.

Here are some suggestions for finding the people who will want to pray for American education:

- Those who have a connection to the US educational system.

- Students involved in intercession for their school.

- Those who desire a change in American education.

- Those with a willingness to work under the direction of the apostle who has jurisdiction over the **Mountain of Education**.

- Intercessors with a knowledge of spiritual warfare.

If you are, or have been, involved in education and the prospect of prayer for education stirs in your spirit, then this call is for you. As the mountain-taking strategy unfolds, the discipline to unite under the apostles and prophets who will implement the strategy will be of vital importance. Everyone will have a part in seeing changes in education develop before our eyes. It will be so revolutionary that we'll wonder, *Why hasn't this been done before?* or *I never imagined that children could learn like this!* We'll see new technologies develop that will astound the world. We'll see new teaching methods that are from God come into the classroom. Godly values will once again be taught and morality will be restored to our nation.

We issue a call to those who are willing to engage in taking the Mountain of Education. Would you take the challenge to take your assignment as a mandate from God to work together under apostolic leadership to take this mountain? Together we can change our nation, one mountain at a time.

When I look back at my experience, if C. Peter Wagner, as an apostle, had not called together that group of professionals over fifteen years ago and asked us to map out our professions, I would have never been exposed to ideas associated with spiritual mapping, which gave me a telescope into the spiritual history of education. We need more apostles who will call different subsets of the church together for projects that will help advance the Kingdom of God.

Most of the apostles whom I have met tend to think only in terms of geographical locations, such as those over cities, states, or nations. But we need God-ordained apostles over each of the seven mountains of influence. A further delineation might be necessary as apostles are identified who are over education in certain locations.

Prayer for Apostolic Prayer Teams

Father, I come to You in the Name of Jesus and ask that You bring Prayer Warriors together to pray for America's educational system. Give them grace to carry out the assignment before them. Let them not be weary in well doing but strengthen them with Your power and might. Let them be one as You and the Father are one. Give them the prayers to pray and the strategy to carry out their assignment. I ask this in Jesus Name. Amen.

19 The Force of A Few

In 1927, physicists Neils Bohr and Werner Heisenberg at the Institute for Theoretical Physics in Copenhagen, Denmark, worked together to determine why particles acted as they do. Their scientific experiments showed that the precise location of a particle is not definite until someone observes it. This presented a problem in that conventional Newtonian physics stated that matter resided in specific locations. Bohr and Heisenberg found that a particle had an infinite number of possible locations that depended on observation. The two scientists discovered what has become known as the **Copenhagen Interpretation**, which states that the simple act of observation is what turns matter into reality. Thus, the study of **quantum physics** was born.

If it is true that we can change one reality to another simply by observation of that reality, then we need to value the way we look at an object, person, or event. Why should we as Christians be surprised at the Bohr and Heisenberg discovery? Jesus told us that we could create a different reality than what we saw with our natural eyes, if we would believe:

"I tell you the truth, if you have faith as small as a mustard seed, you can say to this mountain, 'Move from here to there' and it will move. Nothing will be impossible to you."

Matthew 17:20,21

Perhaps the mustard seed that Jesus was talking about is the focused intention on the desired outcome of any possibility. This kind of mustard seed faith is based on a very solid foundation of leading-edge science, supported by discoveries in quantum physics.

Perhaps the way we view a school or the whole educational system will make a difference in the outcome of the educational mountain. This concept is paramount when getting people to pray for schools. Things are so bad, if we engage in prayer believing that things cannot change, defeat is eminent.

Anyone who prays for a miracle in America's educational system has to look by faith to see our schools differently than the reality of where we are today. Difficult? Absolutely! But it's not impossible!

There may not need to be multiple thousands to pray to make the change, but it will take people with faith to look at the unseen. I've been involved in education for years and there have been times when I've grown weary in the classroom and felt defeated. I can tell you that had I prayed for the whole educational system at that time, frankly, it wouldn't have done a lot of good. That's why it may be a good idea to pass over the weary educator and go for those who are rested and ready for the battle. They can often pray with more faith because they do not know all the detailed problems that exist in the lives of the students, the educators, and a system that has lost its moral compass.

To simply say that we choose a different reality is not enough. We have to believe a different reality. Einstein said, "You cannot solve a problem if you persist in the same reality that created the problem." It is necessary to see a problem differently, in order to change it. That is why Jesus told us to speak to mountains, because focused speaking changes one's reality.

Another discovery in quantum physics is the requirement to jump-start a change in our nation. This is called the creation of a critical mass. *Critical Mass* is when enough people in a community, city, state, or nation adopt a belief or take a certain action; then the whole of the community, city, state, or nation adopts the same belief. Just as we see that the minority of homosexuals in the nation have been able to change the thinking of a lot of people in regard to homosexuality, the same is true of any action that is required to change in our nation.

So, how many people will it take to turn the United States around? Not as many as one might think. Critical mass is determined by taking the square root of 1 percent of the population. According to the 2010 census, the population of the United States was 313,914,040 people. One percent of that number is 3,139,140. Taking the square root of that number, the result is 1,772. According to this, it would take 1,772 people dedicated to a certain outcome.

Imagine, less than 2,000 people dedicated to a certain outcome can produce a major change in our nation. That's why it's important to get people praying the same thing and unified as one in the Holy Spirit, because that's when change happens. The fact that the last prayer Jesus prayed for all believers in the Garden of Gethsemane was for unity lets us know how important it was that the disciples stay together in one mind.

[Jesus said,] "My prayer is not for them alone. I pray also for those who will believe in me through their message, that all of them may be one, Father, just as you are in me and I am in you. May they also be in us so that the world may believe that you have sent me."

John 17:20–21

Unity is the place for miracles.

To create a critical mass of students who would like to see a change in the schools would take considerably less than the 2,000 needed for change in our country. According to the United States Department of Education there are 50,000,000 enrolled in kindergarten through 12th grade in 99,000 schools in this country. One percent of 50,000,000 is 500,000. The square root of 500,000 is 707.1. If only 708 people (because I don't want to fragment that one-tenth of a person) focused on positive change in education, it would be enough to turn our whole system around.

General George Patton was one of the greatest generals who ever commanded US troops. He realized the value of pulling his troops together in unity. During the Battle of the Bulge, when the winter weather was inclement, General Patton ordered a chaplain to write a prayer to God that would change the weather. Once the prayer was composed, General Patton wrote a Christmas card and sent it to all of his troops. On one side of the card was a Christmas greeting that read:

"To each officer and soldier in the Third United States Army, I wish a Merry Christmas. I have full confidence in your courage, devotion to duty, and skill in battle. We march in our might to complete victory. May God's blessings rest upon each of you on this Christmas Day. G.S. Patton, Jr., Lieutenant General, Commanding, Third United States Army."

On the other side of the card was printed the prayer.

"Almighty and most merciful Father, we humbly beseech Thee, of Thy great goodness, to restrain these immoderate rains with which we have had to contend. Grant us fair weather for Battle. Graciously hearken to us as soldiers who call upon Thee that, armed with Thy power, we may advance from victory to victory, and crush the oppression

and the wickedness of our enemies and establish Thy justice among men and nations."[44]

This prayer was sent on December 12, 1944. The weather cleared and the soldiers had the victory. The war was turned because of the victory in that great battle.

General Patton knew the value of getting his soldiers in agreement with him on the request he made to God. Can you imagine a soldier as he read that card in his tent just days before the battle, knowing the danger and the likelihood of defeat if the weather didn't clear before they had to fight the enemy? Patton took his place as a great leader, gave his troops hope, and gave them a point of agreement in the form of a simple Christmas card.

20 Until We Win

The idea of using a few people to make big changes was major strategy of Jesus. First He had His inner circle of Peter, James, and John. The next larger circle was the twelve disciples, the seventy, then the one hundred twenty, and then the masses. Jesus changed the religious nature of the whole world for thousands of years by choosing to disciple twelve men.

Gideon in his fight against the Midianites started with an army of 72,000 men. God instructed him to tell anyone who was fearful to go home. Twenty thousand men remained to fight. At that point, God gave Gideon further instructions to reduce his army. Ultimately 300 men went with Gideon to defeat the Midianites. (Judges 7.) God's reason was that with such a huge army, the credit for the victory would be given to the army by reason of the number of troops. God wanted the credit for the victory to be given to Him.

Across the nation, we see declining test scores, watered down curriculum, a decrease in school attendance, students who graduate without learning to read, just to name a few of the problems we're facing. Then there are the moral issues within the school walls— abortion, bullying, cheating, teachers having sex with their students, and school shootings. The problems stretch like a giant octopus whose tentacles reach even to the smallest community in our country. We all know the system is in trouble but no one knows what to do about it. For the most part, as believers we either take our children out of the system and place them in private schools or we stand on the sidelines and pray for our own children as they face huge temptations the likes of which their grandparents never dreamed. Even those who have no children in school see the decline in the individual integrity of our nation.

Behind all the sin and turmoil we see there is a force of evil bidding for the minds, bodies, and souls of our children and ultimately our nation. Few are aware that the American educational system was set on a negative spiritual course over 100 years ago that has produced the manifestation of decline that we see and experience today in our schools. We must realize that if a spirit of deception is behind the scenes, that spirit can be displaced and replaced by the living God who longs to heal and transform. He is waiting on us to take our place in faith and believe Him for change.

So what do we do? Now is the time for believers to arise like never before in history. pray and believe God for a turnaround in our educational system. It is not too late—it is the perfect time for intercessors to come together.

Often we hear: "These are the last days and 2 Timothy 3 tells us that there will be godlessness in the last days. The world is going to get worse and worse until the Lord returns." This argument is no excuse for letting the enemy run over our children and our nation. Lou Engle, the minister who helped to found International House of Prayer, said, "Don't think that because it is the last days we have to put up with evil!" It is not too late and we, as believers, must never give up.

Could we dream together that education in America could be reformed, transformed, and reborn? That there would be small groups all over this nation—one group in every school, who would be willing to pray together, to bind the strongman over education and to believe God for miracles in the hearts and lives of the students, teachers, support staff, and administrators of their school? Then they would see the big picture and begin to address the root causes of the failure in our schools. Because we know that when two or three people come together in the Name of our Lord Jesus, things will change. It most likely will not be education's elite or powerful who pray, but just people who have faith in God who would believe Him when He said, **"If you ask anything in My name, I will do it." (John 14:14 NKJV).**

It will not take hundreds of thousands of people to make a change in America's education. It will take a few who believe that the system can be changed and who are committed to prayer and in faith can see that the Mountain of Education can be taken and our schools redeemed.

It is possible to change the world one small group at a time. The small group concept used by Jesus is an idea that has seldom been used as a powerful tool to implement cultural change. Some throughout history have used the small group, but it is entirely possible that they just happened on it and never really knew what helped them become successful in what they were trying to accomplish. They just found *a group of like-minded people* and began to meet, talk, and dream together. Once they found that special group, things began to happen...

Jesus chose twelve disciples to spend time with, and those twelve turned the world upside down. (Acts 17:6.) Two thousand years have passed and that rag-tag band of men still exert a tremendous amount of influence through the world. We marvel at the lasting result of the accomplishments of Jesus and the disciples.

Was Jesus on to a *revolutionary idea* when He chose twelve men as His disciples and not one thousand men? What if He gave us a key to changing nations and most of us never truly recognized it as a God idea? We continue to ponder how to gather together large masses of people to bring change. But for the most part, we still haven't got it.

We continue on—hoping for change but not really knowing how to fuel the fires of revival and cultural renewal.

Einstein, early in his career formed a small group who met together to discuss new mathematical formulas and new ideas about how the universe was created. That small group was formed when these men were in their twenties and they remained friends even when they were in their seventies. They were largely responsible for the branch of physics that we now call *quantum physics*.

C. S. Lewis had a small group of men who met on a regular basis to discuss literary ideas. They made literary history by encouraging a body of written works that were thought-provoking and God-revealing.

William Wilberforce and his group of committed friends became known as the **Clapham Circle** because they lived in a community called Clapham. This small group shared a strong belief in Jesus as a personal Savior. They also possessed a shared set of social values derived from the basis of their faith. Within that framework, they shared a commitment to the application of the Gospel to the great social issues of their day. They dared to dream together of how England could be a better place—how they could eradicate slavery, debtor's prisons, child labor, and cruelty to animals (just to name a few). Their meetings were not like ordinary meetings. They centered on worship and prayer, seeking to know the mind of God on the issues that confronted them in their day.

What would happen if we all began to gather in small groups of people who were totally committed to Jesus? Could we dare to dream about how He could bring revival and cultural change to education? If our educational system changed, our whole nation would be a different place.

Transforming the complete educational institution ingrained over the past two hundred years with Socialists' anti-God philosophy is an assignment not for the faint of heart. While it may happen in a short time, intercessors must be prepared for the long haul. Oklahoma City is a stellar example of what intercessors can do when they start on a course and stay on track until transformation is complete.

One of Oklahoma City's darkest days occurred on April 19, 1995, when Timothy McVey bombed the Alfred P. Murrah Federal Building located in the state capitol complex. It was the worst case of domestic terrorism in our country's history prior to September 11, 2001. One hundred sixty-eight people were killed, 680 people were injured, 342 buildings within a 16 block radius were destroyed or damaged.[45] Economically Oklahoma City was already strapped because of the failure of one of its major banks in the 1980s—Penn Square National Bank. The domino effect began as 139 banks followed Penn Square's downfall. Oil, one of Oklahoma City's major industries, began to dry up.

When the US began to import oil from the Middle East, Oklahoma's shallow wells became too expensive to operate. Because of the lack of finances, Oklahoma City's infrastructure was decimated. To add insult to injury, in 2007, *Men's Fitness* magazine ranked Oklahoma City as the 15th fattest city in the nation.

In the early 1990s, John Benefiel looked at the situation and thought, *I see no reason why all of Oklahoma City shouldn't be saved. And if I could believe God for my city, I could believe God for my state. I see in Matthew 6:9–10 that Jesus told us how to pray for our territory.*[46] So he gathered people to pray.

A first effort was to pull together city pastors to pray in unity for the city. The next step was to call people to repentance for all the broken treaties between the US government and the Native Americans. During the period from 1778 until 1883, the United States government ratified more than 370 treaties with the Native Americans. At least another 45 were negotiated but never ratified, although some took legal effect, all of them were broken.[47]

John said, "We repented, we prayed, and we walked the land. Oklahoma City has experienced a dynamic turnaround. Oklahoma

City is now the opposite of the story depicted in the book *Grapes of Wrath*,[48] where Oklahomans fled to California in droves to avoid the poverty and drought. Now Californians are flocking to Oklahoma City because of the great opportunities."

Building from the ground of repentance up, Oklahoma City was transformed and is now known as a destination city where Oklahoma City Mayor Mick Cornett said, "We're building a city where your kid and grandkid are going to choose to live."[49]

When Apostle Benefiel started participating in prayer that would transform Oklahoma City, he met with George Otis Jr. and received what he considers some of the best advice he has gotten as a minister. Otis is the leader of The Sentinel Group, a Christian research and information agency dedicated to helping the Church pray knowledgeably for the end-time global evangelization and enabling communities to discover the pathway to genuine revival and societal transformation. Otis told Benefiel at that meeting, "In order to see a city transformed, you must stay with prayer until the transformation occurs and then pray for sustained transformation. Secondly, you must have fervent united prayer."

I contend that in order to see American education transformed, we must stay with prayer until transformation occurs and then pray for sustained transformation. Secondly, we must have fervent united prayer.

21 Ground Level Strategies

Wlliam J. Seymour is credited with the start of the Pentecostal movement we have today, with a conservative following of 500 million people worldwide and considered the fastest growing movement across the globe. Seymour, the son of a former slave, knew that if speaking in tongues was in the Bible, it was for today. When he read **Acts 2:4, "All of them were filled with the Holy Spirit and began to speak in other tongues as the Spirit enabled them"**—he believed it. The year was 1905. It is said that that Seymour put his head between wooden crates to pray, seldom speaking a word until he heard from God.

The blind received their sight and the lame walked, as numerous miracles occurred at the run-down building on Azusa Street in Los Angeles. Seymour was a rare individual because he learned the power of focus. He knew how to tune his spirit into the Spirit of God and remain there until God moved.

That is exactly what will be required of those who move mountains. They will know the power of focus and how important it is to stay with God until the answer comes. It's simple yet not easy.

But if we have identified the strongman over education and have a strategy for his displacement, we will be able to focus our faith on reformation in our schools.

There are some specific things on which we can agree as we start on our journey.

Speak to Mountains

One of the most profound experiences I ever had speaking to a mountain was in Israel in 2005. I stood at an Israeli outpost that overlooked the two mountains of Gerizim and Ebal. That was where Moses instructed the Israelites to be divided. Half of the tribes stood on Mount Ebal to pronounce curses for any disobediences of God's laws. The other half stood on Mount Gerizim to pronounce blessings. (Deuteronomy 27:11–13.) Nestled between Gerizim and Ebal is the ancient city of Shechem. The day I was there Shechem was under Israeli military observation for harboring a Hamas terrorist cell.

With our guide looking on, my friends Donna, Pat, and I prayed for Israel by pronouncing the same blessing that Moses had instructed the Israelites to speak as recorded in Deuteronomy 28. We yelled the blessings out across the valley with our hands stretched toward Mount Ebal and Mount Gerizim. Then we spoke Psalm 91. As we made declarations and spoke the Word of God over the mountains and the valley, something happened in the realm of the Spirit. We felt the atmosphere change as if charged with negative ions. The smell became fresh. Something had been released in the Spirit.

The next day on CNN news, I saw a ticker run across the bottom of the screen. "Eleven terrorists captured in the city of Shechem hidden behind a false toilet door." I ran to tell my friends. Donna and I left the hotel immediately to find a copy of the *Jerusalem Post*, excited that the newspaper documented the answer to prayer.

Did our prophetic declarations have anything to do with the capture of the terrorists? I believe they did. How many more adventures does God have for us if we will learn to go to strategic places, speak to mountains, and make prophetic declarations? Once you've seen a mountain move, something happens in your faith that will change you forever. You become a person of destiny, with spiritual strength, determined to root out the enemy. Nothing short of victory will ever satisfy. That day in Israel, I learned a lesson on how to take a mountain.

Jesus was explicit in His instructions to us when we face mountains of obstacles. He told us to SPEAK to mountains and they would move. He not only told us once but three times in the Gospels. I list those scriptures here because learning to speak to mountains is an important prayer strategy—one that is vastly underused.

Matthew 17:20–21—He replied, "Because you have so little faith. I tell you the truth, *if you have faith as small as a mustard seed, you can say to this mountain*, 'Move from here to there' and it will move. Nothing will be impossible for you," (emphasis mine).

Matthew 21:21–22—Jesus replied, "I tell you the truth, if you have faith and do not doubt, not only can you do what was done to the fig tree, *but also you can say to this mountain*, 'Go, throw yourself into the sea,' and it will be done. If you believe, you will receive whatever you ask for in prayer," (emphasis mine).

Mark 11:22–24—"Have faith in God," Jesus answered. "I tell you the truth, *if anyone says to this mountain*, 'Go, throw yourself into the sea,' and does not doubt in his heart but believes that what he says will happen, it will be done for him. Therefore I tell you, whatever you ask for in prayer, believe that you have received it, and it will be yours," (emphasis mine).

For years, during my prayer time I wrote out the scriptures that pertained to my situation, prayed over each request, and I had some success. While this was a good exercise, it wasn't what Jesus told me to do. His instruction was to speak to the mountains.

Have you ever wondered why Jesus told us to speak to a mountain? It really made no sense to me until I began to read the new discoveries in quantum physics. The instruction to speak to a mountain is actually on the very leading-edge of science, supported by the discoveries of quantum physics. It is our act of coming together in unity and consciously believing that a mountain can be moved that locks that possibility of the mountain actually moving into reality.

Earlier we talked about Neils Bohr. Some of the beginning experiments in quantum physics performed by him in Denmark in the 1920s proved that the outcome of an experiment is determined by the observer. This is the same as when we expect or believe something to be true while we are observing the reality of the situation. We are experiencing the outcome before it happens. In the quantum realm of possibilities, the mountain has no choice—it must move.

When we by faith speak to a mountain, we are releasing sound waves into the atmosphere that will change the course of nature, whether that mountain is education, religion, family, media, business, arts, or government. Perhaps it's a healing, a financial need, a need for reformation in our country—it doesn't matter. Sound waves are powerful and create another dimension that science is just now discovering. It was the discovery of a weird reaction in subatomic particles called *nonlocality,* which referred to the ability of an electronic entity such as an individual electron to influence another quantum particle instantaneously over any distance despite there being no exchange of force or energy. This meant that the world existed as a complex web of interdependent relationships, forever indivisible.

There is no empty space. All space is filled with particles and cannot be divided into independently existing units or things. When we speak out into the atmosphere, the words we speak are powerful. The prophet Isaiah revealed that thousands of years ago:

As the rain and the snow come down from heaven, and do not return to it without watering the earth and making it bud and flourish, so that it yields seed for the sower and bread for the eater, so is my word that goes out from my mouth; it will not return to me empty, but will accomplish what I desire and achieve the purpose for which I sent it. Isaiah 55: 10,11

We are all connected and the words we speak hit the target.

Speaking to mountains requires that we:

See beyond the mountain. Mountains restrict a view. We cannot see beyond natural problems in a mountain so huge as our educational system, therefore we tend to see them as immovable.

See the mountain as level ground. That means that we assume the position that the mountain has already crumbled. Denial? No, but faith that the problems in our educational system are not stopping us from going forward; only if we draw back and do not address the mountain will we be stopped.

Have mustard seed faith. Mustard seed faith does not refer to a small amount of faith. Anyone who has the audacity to speak to a mountain of influence has to have a lot of faith. I believe that when Jesus talked about mustard seed faith, He was referring to focused faith—so focused that all it can produce is the desired result.

Know who we are in Christ Jesus. Weakness and ineffectiveness plague those who do not know what Jesus has done for us and what His death and resurrection has accomplished.

Know we are designed to be mountain movers! We are destined for this time. Our schools need a change and we will speak that change into being. Francis Frangipane, in his book *This Day We Fight!*, said, "He [God] has called intercessors not to wonder about the future, but to create it through the knowledge of His Living Word and prayer!"[50]

22 Prayers of Agreement

James P. Moore in his book, *One Nation Under God: The History of Prayer in America*, unfolds the history of America from the 1600s as revealed through written prayers. I had never realized the value of written prayers until I saw the inspiration and the faith behind the prayers of a people who forged this new nation called America. A clear faith in the God of our Lord Jesus Christ was the central theme of each prayer. However, as Moore progressed through the centuries, the prayers he shared took a marked turn, and not for the better.

As he researched the 1960s, he found fewer written prayers to reference. Instead of written prayers, he cited the lyrics of America's pop culture and other written words of activists. While they were not really prayers, they were the closest to prayers that he could find. He cited the lyrics of songs sung by Janis Joplin, a famous 60s rock star who died of a drug overdose. Prayers of social activists like Cesar Chavez, who fought for social justice among the vegetable growers in California, were also cited. Chavez's prayer, known as Cesar's Prayer, says in part: "Show me the suffering of the most miserable;

So I will know my people's plight. Free me to pray for others; For you are present in every person..."[51]

Moore found no prayers of significance that mentioned God from a Christian perspective and none prayed to God in the Name of Jesus. What he found were prayers to the Universe and for the most part secular. They were indicative of the turn our country had taken toward secularism. Even the Charismatic movement, which had powerful revival in the 1960s, did not give us written prayers.

Our leaders, with the exception of President Ronald Reagan, did not pray public prayers and especially prayers to the God and Father of our Lord Jesus Christ. There was a fear that came over our officials—of being ridiculed and prosecuted because of openly declaring a faith in Jesus. We must start someplace to redeem our nation and written prayers will record how history was altered because intercessors prayed.

Written prayers allow us to:

1. *Come together in agreement.* Jesus said, **"Again, I tell you that if two of you on earth agree about anything you ask for, it will be done for you by my Father in heaven. For where two or three come together in my name, there am I with them,"** (Matthew 18:19–20).

2. *Clarify exactly the end result of your faith.* Have you ever tried to write out a prayer? It's not as easy as it sounds. But writing helps us to clarify exactly the results we believe will happen.

3. *Measurable results.* When General Patton needed the weather to clear so his men could land at Normandy, he wrote a prayer and sent it with a Christmas card to his troops. All of his men prayed the same prayer and came in agreement. God answered, the weather cleared, and the allied forces won the Battle of Normandy.

To see education change, intercessors must focus, come together in unity, and know the end result we desire.

23 Praying the Word of God

There are approximately 4 million teachers in the American public school system[52] and many of whom are believers. The tipping point, or critical mass, for change would be 200 teachers. That's not a huge number, but the secret is that this number has to be in complete unity. If 200 teachers all prayed in their classrooms, in one day, the results could be astounding. But teachers are trained to remain secular in their classrooms. They walk a daily tightrope to be politically correct and free of offense to any religion.

In the teaching profession, every teacher suffers his or her share of attacks as a usual routine of events. They assign too much homework and parents complain. They don't stay after school to tutor those who were having trouble learning algebra. (Never mind that they may offer their services at noon for free tutoring every day.) They get in trouble for expecting projects and homework to be turned in on time because, after all, what has a deadline got to do with learning a subject? If the student did the work, why shouldn't they get credit, even if it was late? The list goes on and on and every teacher who has ever tried to do his or her best has come under attack. These skirmishes erode the soul of teachers leaving them little energy to fight the big battles that change the system.

Teachers live in fear of being fired for praying over a student or even for putting up Christmas decorations in a classroom. They have no strength for losing a job over something as simple as ministering to a child. Getting a teacher to see the big battle when he or she is fighting multiple little battles every day is difficult. That is why we haven't seen the critical mass we need to see for the change. A unified core mass is what we need and we need it now.

If Christian teachers unified to such an extent that they could define small actions that would change the system, the tipping point could happen. Malcolm Gladwell in his book *The Tipping Point: How Little Things Can Make a Big Difference* shares his research into what will make changes in society.[53] Gladwell proposes that it is the little things that make a big difference.

Liberal educators make claims that our schools are in such a state of decline because we don't have enough money for education or because our students are economically impoverished. They say that if we just had more money for new curriculum or if we would just make sure that everyone has money, either through welfare or through giving someone a job, that would be the best way to create better schools. But there is another factor involved that Gladwell calls **"The Power of Context,"** which states that it's really the little things that matter.

For instance, the crime turnaround in New York City occurred, not because of a huge war on crime, but because of what has become known as the "Broken Windows Theory." This theory was the brainchild of two criminologists—James Q. Wilson and George Kelling. Wilson and Kelling argued that crime is a result of disorder. If a broken window in a house in a crime-ridden part of town is not repaired, the result is that more criminal elements will be attracted to that neighborhood and the crime rate will rise substantially. There will be more houses with broken windows. Drug dealers will move into the neighborhood and there is a general feeling that the neighborhood is bad and the crime rate skyrockets. Fix the broken windows, Wilson and Kelling said, and the bad elements will abandon the neighborhood. They believed that crime was contagious.

New York City tipped when the police began to issue citations for broken windows, giving owners twenty-four hours to make repairs. Graffiti also was cleaned up within twenty-four hours of when the artful designers had completed their work of art.

What if educational administrators and teachers began to do little things like pray with students, openly display scriptures in their classrooms, or refuse to call Christmas holidays by the secular name winter holidays? The educational system can tip in the direction of being restored back to a Godly system if enough administrators and teachers would aggressively live out their Christian faith.

24 Approaching the Court of Heaven

You must have a desire to change American education, or you wouldn't have picked up this book. If your interest has been piqued, now you probably want to know: "Do we have the right to claim the whole American education system for the Kingdom of God? After all, education is secular and appeals to the mind of man." That's true, but education includes not only the mind but also the spirit. We currently have a system that tries to educate only the mind to the exclusion of the spirit of man and the system isn't working.

The test scores in the United States have plummeted over the past fifty years along with the moral climate of our schools. The first schools in America were founded by godly men and women who educated their children to not only have head knowledge but to have a moral compass that would allow them to be good children, parents, and citizens.

The courts of our day have used the legal system set up by our forefathers to tear down the fundamental beliefs of our country. In November 2008, the citizens of California voted to ban marriages between persons of the same sex. A case to challenge the ban was brought before the US Supreme Court and in 2013, the Supreme Court ruled against the ban. Homosexual and lesbian marriages were allowed, regardless of how the people voted.

In 1962, the US Supreme Court handed down the ruling that would no longer permit prayer in public schools. In the case, *Engle vs. Vitale*, the court rendered a ruling which declared that it was not the state's place to promote religion in schools. The court used the separation of church and state clause that many believe to be in our Constitution. The phrase ***Separation of Church and State*** appears in a personal letter Thomas Jefferson wrote to Danbury Baptist Church in Connecticut and assured the Danbury Church that there would never be a national denomination in America.

The Supreme Court has rendered many rulings that eliminated practices that made our country great. We have had to stand by and watch as rulings by the highest court of our nation have taken away our foundational freedoms. It is time that we learn our legal rights, perhaps not in the sense that we need to go to a university to become a lawyer but in the sense that we need to know our legal rights before God. If we take the Mountain of Education back, we will need to do so in the Courts of Heaven. We will have to take our place before God, stand our ground, and speak to the Mountain.

It is precisely because we have lost so much moral ground in our earthly court system that God is bringing the teaching on how to enter in the Courts of Heaven to reclaim our rights. As believers, we are kings and priests. Peter says, **"You are a chosen people, a royal priesthood, a holy nation, a people belonging to God, that you may declare the praises of him who called you out of darkness into his wonderful light,"**
(1 Peter 2:9).

We are called to make a difference in this earth. Man is God's legal agent and access to earth. We were put here to claim and reclaim territory for God. If we do not enter into our divine destiny, those who do not serve our God will take the initiative to claim territory for Satan.

Robert Henderson in his book *Interceding in the Courts of Heaven* has great information on how we are to pray before God in a legal capacity. I highly recommend that you read his book. Also, because we have a legal right to claim our educational system, we will use legal documents to divorce Baal and to execute a Writ of Assistance, a legal document asking God for assistance from heaven in claiming what is rightfully ours. We will present these petitions before the Courts of Heaven to gain ground and reclaim what has wrongfully been taken from us. We can come before God and make our petitions. The apostle Paul says, **"Let us then approach the throne of grace with confidence, so that we may receive mercy and find grace to help us in our time of need"** **(Hebrews 4:16).**

25 Historical Entry Points

Many people rally around the issue of restoring prayer back in schools and believe that all our educational ills would be resolved if we could just start prayer in the classrooms. For this group of people, the year 1962 was the turning point when our schools started their decline. Pointing to this one single incident leaves us a bit shortsighted in understanding the causes of our problems. School prayer being eliminated is the only thing that those of us in this present generation can remember and while it was a significant undoing in our system, it certainly was not the most crucial incident, or the first.

We are like a family that entertained a guest, not one we particularly liked, but we put up with for many years. In fact, we allowed that guest to stay so long on our property that they obtained squatter's rights. We never realized the severity of what happened until one day the sheriff showed up to tell us that our guests had claimed half of the farm and while we could continue to till the land, we just couldn't plant any seeds without our guest's permission.

In the same light, we have allowed the enemy squatter's rights in our schools. We can't plant seeds of the Gospel in the lives of our students. We lost our rights and now we are the outsiders. We do have the right to take the squatters into the **Courts of Heaven**, prove that they were deceptive, and demand they give back our territory.

The educational system in America has undergone numerous changes since its inception in the 1600s. A look back over the last 400 years of written history will give the discerning believer a clear view of decisions that have been made in the educational system that determine the rise and fall of the United States of America as a nation. Some of the most devastating situations in our system demonstrate demonic activity at its height, but have their roots in decisions made early in our country's history by men and women of influence who promoted a system of thought contrary to God's. However much good they proposed at the time, history has proven that some of the doors they opened allowed evil to influence our children's minds and has led our educational structure down a self-destructive path.

I have identified ten major historical entry points that gave the enemy entrance into American education. Along with the identification of each entry point, I explain why I believe that event is important, which includes the spiritual significance of the event, the place of physical repentance, along with prayers and prophetic declarations for each.

With proper understanding intercessors have a unique advantage in prayer and faith as we stand before God to change our schools. Change is imminent, maybe not in the exact way we prescribe, but things will change when we pray. God can restore our schools and replace those who make ungodly policies that affect our children. God's changes will reflect His sovereignty but will not make our classrooms look like they did fifty years ago. He will do a new work, but it will be more effective than what we could think or imagine. Will Christians take their place in prayer and spiritual warfare and go before God on behalf of a system that literally holds the minds of the youth of our country in bondage to a false system that perverts their thinking and renders them as spiritually impotent citizens? We have no other hope but in God. Our prayer is like that of Jehoshaphat's as he prayed when Judah and Jerusalem faced great armies threatening to defeat them.

"O our God, will you not judge them? For we have no power to face this vast army that is attacking us. We do not know what to do, but our eyes are upon you... As they began to sing and praise, the LORD set ambushes against the men of Ammon and Moab and Mount Seir who were invading Judah, and they were defeated... The fear of God came upon all the kingdoms of the countries when they heard how the LORD had fought against the enemies of Israel... And the kingdom of Jehoshaphat was at peace, for his God had given him rest on every side."

2 Chronicles 20:12,22,29–30)

In Genesis 18:16–33, Abraham dialogued with God in order to spare the city of Sodom. Abraham asked that the city to be spared if there were ten righteous men there. It's a pity that ten people didn't step up to the plate and pray on behalf of those cities. There may be a few believers who might gloat over the destruction of two powerful cities, but I believe the majority of us feel sad that so many people were destroyed because of a lack of intercessors.

Daniel's prayer of repentance recorded in Daniel 9 gives guidelines for prayer to intercede for our schools:

"Now, our God, hear the prayers and petitions of your servant. For your sake, O Lord, look with favor on your desolate sanctuary. Give ear, O God, and hear; open your eyes and see the desolation of the city that bears your Name. We do not make requests of you because we are righteous, but because of your great mercy. O Lord, listen! O Lord, forgive! O Lord, hear and act! For your

sake, O my God, do not delay, because your city and your people bear your Name. While I was speaking and praying, confessing the sin and the sin of my people Israel and making my request to the Lord my God for his holy hill—while I was still in prayer, Gabriel, the man I had seen in the earlier vision came to me in swift flight about the time of the evening sacrifice."

Daniel 9:17–21

As Daniel prayed and confessed the sins of his people, Gabriel came to him with an answer. I believe God is waiting for His people to become serious about our school system and stand in prayer and ask for forgiveness for the past sins that have taken place and ask for help for the future. God can and will intervene if His people will pray. His promise to us in 2 Chronicles 7:14 says, "If my people, who are called by my Name, will humble themselves and pray and seek my face and turn from their wicked ways, then will I hear from heaven...and will heal their land."

God's promise to us is healing. Our duty to Him is prayer.

26 Prayer and Repentance

Once I began the process of spiritual mapping the educational system, my eyes were opened to the possibility of praying at a new level to promote change that surfaces like a bubbling stream. Spiritual mapping led me to ten major entry points where the enemy was allowed into our educational system. It would be important for a prayer team to travel to each of those entry points to pray, just as my friend Roberta had done at the twenty most evil sights in the world. The prayer team would address why our educational system isn't as effective as is should be.

At each site, they would deal with the ancient roots of iniquity that have found their way into our educational system through decisions made by our leaders. At each site the prayer team would read the Baal divorce decreed, pray and make prophetic declarations.

Historical Entry Points are locations where the enemy gained access to our educational system, and are strategic prayer sites for prayer. Prayer at the historical locations is like interceding for a country while visiting it. Praying on site at a public school is the equivalent of praying for a country at the site of their embassy. The land an embassy is built on is legally the sovereign soil of the country the embassy represents. There are approximately 100,000 public schools in America. Wouldn't it be wonderful if intercessors would go to each school in the nation and pray on site?

When you visit a school site, here are a few helpful hints:

1. Obtain permission, if necessary, to pray at the school. One group of intercessors has prayed at a school for over ten years. They pray on Saturday and before they start they make sure the janitor knows they are walking around the school and praying. If you pray during school hours, check in at the school office if necessary or meet with the principal. Do whatever it takes to make sure those in authority at the school know you are there and why.

2. If at all possible, start at the flagpole. The flagpole is easily found and is a good place to begin.

3. Make all your prayers and confessions for the school positive. It is easy to pick up on the negatives around a school. Everyone brings the sum total of all his or her experiences to school and sensitive intercessors can sense the negative and also the anti-God atmosphere around a school. It's easy to get distracted so tune out distractions and stay focused in His Praises and Confessions.

4. After you have read the Divorce Decree, confess the Word over the school. Speak to the areas in the spirit realm that you want changed. It is always appropriate to pray scriptures in every situation.

5. End your time in praise.

27 Trans Generational Prayer

One of the most powerful prayer meetings in history was conducted by five college students. Their prayers literally changed the course of history and the effects are felt today. The movement sparked by this small group is known as the beginning of Protestant missions. In August 1806, five students from Williams College in Williamstown, Massachusetts, met in a grove of trees near the Hoosic River, in what was then known as Sloan's Meadow.

Their purpose was to discuss their concern for the people of Asia and the theology of missionary service. Suddenly their meeting was interrupted by a thunderstorm causing the students to take immediate shelter under a haystack until the sky cleared. One of the students later related, "The brevity of the shower, the strangeness of the place of refuge, and the peculiarity of their topic of prayer and conference all took hold of their imaginations and their memories."[54] And take hold it did.

The 1806 meeting is considered the beginning of the missions movement in this country. Those five students changed the course of missions that is still having an impact on the world today. Samuel John Mills went on to found **The American Bible Society** and the

United Foreign Missionary Society. Others taking refuge in that haystack founded the **American Board of Commissioners for Foreign Missions**, and the first missions publication, the *Missionary Herald*, was a result of the Haystack Revival.

Some of the most powerful prayer meetings I have ever attended were ones where students interceded, often with agonizing groans, for their fellow students. Their intense concern for their peers provoked everyone to pray for a lost generation whom our educational system has ill-served.

Beth Nimo, Rachel Scott's mother, once told me that she had taken Rachel to the doctor with intense stomach pains. After Rachel was murdered in the 1999 Columbine High School shootings, Beth reflected that most likely Rachel's pains were the result of an intense burden of intercession because she cared deeply about the spiritual condition of her classmates.

To join across generational lines with young people like Rachel who have a deep desire to see their generation know Jesus is to create a powerful synergy of generational intercession and healing for the youth of our land. It is vitally important that we link adults with the youth for trans-generational prayer to transform our schools and our nation.

28 Native Americans and African Americans in Education

Negiel Bigpond is a well-respected member of the Euchee Tribe in Oklahoma. Several years ago I asked him to come to **A City-Wide Call to Pray for Education** meeting my organization, **Teach the Children International**, was hosting. Our guest speaker was Beth Nimo, the mother of Rachel Scott who was murdered in the 1999 Columbine High School massacre. Negiel graciously accepted my invitation. I will never forget the impact as he came to the lectern at the end of a very emotional meeting where Beth had shared her daughter's legacy of faith to see her classmates come to know Jesus. Many in the audience were already openly weeping.

Negiel lifted his hands toward heaven as though the audience were a part of a solemn Euchee ceremony and said, *"I pronounce that a Warring Spirit of Prayer to descend on everyone here. Each will know how to war in the spirit for the children of this nation."* The only sound in the auditorium was of weeping. Negiel slowly stepped down from the stage. It was the shortest benediction and the most powerful I had ever witnessed and I'm sure I wasn't the only one who had felt the intensity of what had been spoken. No one could have spoken more powerfully or with more authority. As a Native American, Negiel had commissioned an audience of several hundred people to pray in a reformation for our children. The words he spoke were powerful and effective.

In my search for the root causes of what went awry with our system, one of my first efforts was to look for elders of First Nations who would give me insight as to what they thought we should do at this point to turn the system back to God.

Many schools were set up for Native Americans when our nation was in its infancy. Harvard, established in 1636, received funds that helped secure the survival of the institution during its beginning years from the London-based organization the Society for the Propagation of the Gospel in New England, also known as the New England Company. The donations were sent to educate and convert Indians. Moor's Charity School (later Dartmouth College) offered an education to Indians as early as 1617. In 1774, William and Mary College invited their Indian neighbors to attend their college. The Indians declined William and Mary's offer stating that previous youth who had been educated in college came back to the tribe as, unskilled in tribal ways and basically good for nothing."[55]

The Harvard charter of 1650 describes its mission as "the education of the English and Indian youth of this country." An Indian youth who attended Harvard, also received an education from a college for Indians, where the first Indian Bible and many other Christian books for Native Americans were published.[56]

Dealing with Root Causes

From the beginning, education of an Indian child involved the removal of the child from his or her family and all other familiar surroundings. The child would then be placed in a boarding school, which was a complete change in his environment and one for which he was ill-suited. This may have been the reason why few of the

Indians survived their educations. The Indian youths were not accustomed to the rigors of sitting for hours on end in order to study for a classical education like that offered at Harvard.

Negiel Bigpond's Euchee Tribe is a part of the Creek Nation. Born and raised in Oklahoma, Negiel is unique in that he is a fourth generation believer. I asked to talk with Negiel to get his thoughts on education from the perspective of a First Nations person. "The First Nation's People considered themselves to be keepers of land," Negiel explained. "We were not 'possessors of the land' like the Europeans" Negiel continued, " I find that the more I travel and talk with Native Americans there is a deep-seated resentment for the boarding schools that were set up by the white men. In those schools, there were a lot of deaths and defilements of our children. There is such bitterness that it will take time to heal, but we must start the healing process. **The roots of those educational attempts are like open wounds that need to be healed.**"

My first thought was that apologies to the First Nations had already been offered and we were well into the beginning stages of the healing process. After a bit of research, I found that was not the case. An official apology was secretly signed by President Barack Obama on Saturday, December 19, 2009, without any press allowed to attend the signing. The President never publicly acknowledged the apology. After much effort and five years after he started the initiative, the originator of the Resolution, Senator Sam Brownback (R-KS), had the bill added to the Defense Appropriations Act, H.R. 3326.

On May 20, 2010, Senator Brownback publically read the apology at an event at the Congressional Cemetery in Washington, D.C. with five tribal leaders present. It was clear that the apology had not reached its full impact because the President didn't fully acknowledge the United States' mistreatment of the First Nations people and the lack of national participation in the apology. There is more work to do to complete the apology process.

Canada, on the other hand, took a different approach. On Wednesday, June 11, 2008, Prime Minister Stephen Harper asked Canada's 30 million citizens to pause to participate in an unprecedented public apology to their First Nations and their indigenous peoples. Since that time, Canada has experienced a financial turnaround. The United States has not.

Dr. Bigpond was right in his assessment that the root cause of the resentment in this country has not been dealt with properly. Perhaps we can start to address this problem with prayer for a public apology, especially as it relates to relocation of Native American children to boarding schools. The US had over 100 of those residential schools, and some are still in operation today.

The boarding schools were a part of the European mindset, which gave the newcomers the oversight advantage. The Europeans saw themselves as "possessors of the land" instead of the Native Americans. As possessors, they wanted to take care of the people and educate the children. In order to see after their new charges, they removed the children from the homes. Treaties were signed and almost as quickly as they were signed they were broken. Education was one more agreement the new settlers had with the First Nations that didn't work. Instead of allowing the children to remain in their homes and introducing the Bible, they chose family separation. The purpose ultimately was not the education in and of itself but to change the child's world view, a tactic that has been implemented throughout history.

Today we see the effects founding educators like Horace Mann and John Dewey had on our education system—men who sought to separate American children from the influence of their families and the church by isolating them from all vestiges of Christianity by the removal of all Christian references in public school curricula in order to separate the church from the state.

Another blight in our more recent history that needs to be addressed is the banning of African-American students from our public schools in the 1950s and 1960s. I was in junior high at the time and only remember sketches of news, which was amazing because I lived in southern Arkansas.

One of the first instances of banning happened in 1957 at Little Rock Central High School in Little Rock, Arkansas, when nine African-American students enrolled in the school. My parents were of the opinion that the schools were public and everyone who lived in the school district should be allowed to attend a neighborhood school. It was not a topic that was up for discussion at our dinner table. That's probably why I don't remember it being a big deal, but those who were offended viewed it differently.

Today many of the school districts that have a high African-American enrollment suffer because no one has dealt with the ancient thrones of iniquity that still wields authority over these students. The spirit of poverty, fatherlessness, abandonment, and subordination are major issues. As intercessors, we will not leave any child uncovered by our prayers. We will repent for this time in our history when many of our children were denied access to equal education and we will declare victory over all the children.

Prayer of Repentance to First Nations People

Father, I come to You in the Name of Jesus repenting for the mistreatment of the First Nation's children, when they were placed in boarding schools. I ask for an apology to come from the highest office of this land, the President of the United States. I also ask that the President call the whole nation to repentance.

Father, we have caused your little ones to sin, and you said that it would be better that a millstone were hung around our neck and we be thrown into the sea. (Luke 17:2.) We ask your forgiveness and mercy on our country. Restore those we have offended and let healing flow like a river through America. I pray this in the Name of Jesus. Amen

Prayer of Repentance for Denying African-American Children
Equal Access to Schools

Father, in the Name of Jesus I come to You and ask for repentance for our nation for denying any child equal access to our educational system. I bind the spirit of rejection over our children and ask that all children know their importance in this nation as well as in the Kingdom of God. Let our doors be open and our hearts be ready to receive these children You bring to our schools. I bind the spirit of fatherlessness, poverty, destruction, and isolation. I loose a spirit of love, unity, and cooperation. Give us great understanding and wisdom on how to educate every child. Amen

29 Entry Point # 1: Harvard Takeover

The takeover of Harvard in 1805 by the Unitarians is one of the most significant events in history in regard to the spiritual climate of our country's intellectuals. Harvard was founded by the Calvinists in 1636 with the intent that it would be a fortress of Christian education. Harvard's student body was to be comprised of clergy candidates and Native American Indians who, when educated, would take the message of salvation to this new country. English mission agencies gave donations to Harvard to underwrite the cost of the education of the American Indian students.

If there were any doubt about Harvard's original intent, those would be dispelled by Harvard's motto adopted in 1692—*Veritas Christo et Ecclesiae*, which translated from Latin means "Truth for Christ and the Church." The motto, sometime in the twentieth century, was later changed to simply *Veritas* or "Truth." The change indicated Harvard's change to an era of reasoning rather than continuing on its original Christian foundation.

The founding fathers of Harvard followed in the footsteps of the Reformation and were even called Calvinists because they followed the doctrines of John Calvin, the famous French theologian who led the Reformation in France and in Switzerland. As believers in a salvation experience that came through faith in the work that Jesus accomplished on the cross, they were strong and determined. They started Harvard with a vision to train ministers and Native American Indians, but the battle for the minds of the youth of this country proved to be a tough one that the Calvinists would eventually lose.

On the opposite side of the belief scale were the Unitarians, who believed that man was basically good and saw no need of being justified by faith. The Unitarians were dissatisfied and felt the students at Harvard could be best served by being free of the confines of a restrictive religion. New ideas were flowing freely from the bright minds that assembled regularly in the parlors and meeting rooms of Europe. The discussions consisted of the latest thoughts and suppositions that were a part of the enlightened age. Slowly those new thoughts spread across to the newly discovered continent of America.

Unitarians embraced a new thought that was really as old as time, that education could be geared to improve man's character and when man became educated he would become moral and all social injustices would be eliminated.

Years before the takeover, many of America's brightest minds from Harvard traveled to Germany to study the philosophy of Georg Friedrich Hegel. They embraced the new thought that everything in the universe was on an equal footing with God. Everything was seen as subject to evolution—a man's mind, our customs, social concepts, and our cultures. The universe was progressing toward perfection. (One of Hegel's best known disciples was Karl Marx.) Unitarian professors at Harvard accepted Hegel's philosophy and began to integrate these ideas into their teaching.

Initially, they met with resistance since most of the students came from a reformed background. In order to accomplish a takeover of the institution, the new thinkers reasoned that it would be best to focus on a takeover of the Harvard Board of Directors and then work to hire more enlightened professors.

A bitter struggle ensued but eventually the board of Harvard was taken over by the Unitarians, settling the question of the emphasis that would be promoted in the Harvard classrooms and in the hiring process of new professors. The new hires would be products of the age of reasoning, **enlightened** in their thinking, imparting this new philosophy to their students. In the context of the classroom the change was gradual, yet over the years Harvard became a school that would influence the world—but not in the context of the beliefs of the Founding Fathers.

One classic example of Harvard's digression was expressed by Chester M. Pierce, MD, a professor of education and psychiatry at Harvard, who in 1903 told educators at the Childhood International Education Seminar in Denver:

"Every child in America entering school at the age of 5 is mentally ill because he comes to school with certain allegiances to our founding fathers, toward our elected officials, toward his parents, toward a belief in a supernatural being, and toward the sovereignty of this nation as a separate entity. It's up to you as teachers to make all these sick children well—by creating the international child of the future."[57]

Harvard, once a fortress for Christ and the Church, had fallen into the hands of the progressives, which is where it remains today.

Why Is This Entry Point Significant?

Harvard was not the only American university to fall under the influence of the belief that man's mind was supreme and would lead him to God, but it was the first! Neither is it the only school that started with a Godly board of directors who would eventually be voted out of office and replaced. Often the new board members are those with the latest and greatest ideas that appeal to the intellect and exclude salvation by grace and moral teaching based on Biblical principles. This type of humanistic teaching in its appeal to the mind alone promotes the doctrines of socialism and communism.

Professors who rely only on man's reasoning squelch the independent thinking of children who sit in classrooms under their teachings. Eventually these children lose their ability to think independently. The end result is a departure from the belief of the ability to have a personal relationship with God. **Proverbs 14:12 certainly applies: "There is a way that seems right to a man, but in the end it leads to death."** Our country was founded by men who valued a person's independence. Submitting to reasoning as a way of life was the death of freedom.

Since education apart from God places more emphasis on the mind than the spirit of a man, the progression to liberal, godless ideas that feed the mind but not the spirit take place. Many schools like Harvard, Princeton, Yale, and Columbia were all started by churches with religious charters and later became secular. In American education, when these two worldviews clash, the secularists usually win.

Many Christian private schools in the twenty-first century have separated from the umbrella of the founding church only to be liberalized. Often it is the desire of the parents that causes the separation. Parents see the church as too controlling and the policies too restrictive and seek to separate the school from the church. If they can gain positions on the school board, pressure can be put on the church to separate the religious teaching from the curriculum of the school.

Many advocates of the separation rely on the Christian charter of the school as a safeguard against liberalism. The argument is that a school charter based on Godly principles will sustain the spiritual environment of the school, but history has not proven that to be the case, as we saw with Harvard and their motto that once said, **"Truth for Christ and the Church"** and now only says **"Truth."** As with water, education without restraints will seek the lowest level, and that will be humanism. The end result of educating only the mind is that the neglected spirit wants more and more degrees of separation from God. The spiritual vacuum created in a humanistic educational institution is quickly filled with liberal teaching.

Harvard's takeover was of utmost importance because it was the first Christian institution of higher learning to fall. Harvard had, and still has, intellectual collateral. Graduates from Harvard command a great deal of respect and degrees from the school are revered. Harvard set an example that other schools would want to follow. After all, if Harvard became secular, then why wouldn't every other college in America want to follow their example? It would only require less than fifty humanistic teachers at the top of the Harvard ladder to get the ball rolling.

What Happened in the Realm of the Spirit?

Once Harvard was removed from under the authority of born-again Christians, the board of directors was able to introduce curriculum, teachers, and ideas that promoted the enlightened ideals that professors from Harvard learned as they traveled Europe. The Age of Enlightenment was a period in the seventeenth and eighteenth centuries that began in Europe and later spread to the American colonies.

The movement was sparked by philosophers John Locke (1632–1704), Voltaire (1694–1778), and physicist Isaac Newton (1643–1727). The ideas that spread to this new land promoted the theory that enlightened people would reform society using reason—they would challenge ideas grounded in tradition and faith, and advance knowledge through the scientific method. It promoted scientific thought, skepticism, and intellectual interchange and opposed superstition, intolerance, and abuses of power by the church and the state. The ideas of the Enlightenment have had a major impact on the culture, politics, and government, not only of the United States, but also of the Western world.

The apostle Paul said:

I am astonished that you are so quickly deserting the one who called you by the grace of Christ and are turning to a different gospel— which is really no gospel at all. Evidently some people are throwing you into confusion and are trying to pervert the gospel of Christ. But even if we or an angel from heaven should preach a gospel other than the one we preached to you, let him be eternally condemned!

Galatians 1:6–8

Paul was so emphatic about staying with the Gospel of Christ that he repeated himself in verse 9, "As we have already said, so now I say again: if anybody is preaching to you a gospel other than what you accepted, let him be eternally condemned!"

Certainly the people of America were delivered another god that would bring them to a place of depravity as we see today in our schools.

Samuel Blumenfeld in his book, *NEA: Trojan Horse in American Education* wrote:

"…probably the most important [event] in American history: the takeover of Harvard by the Unitarians in 1805 and the expulsion of the Calvinists. That takeover not only made Harvard the citadel of religious and moral liberalism, but also the citadel of anti-Calvinism. Once the significance of that event is understood, the intellectual history of America suddenly begins to make much more sense, for no event has had a greater long-range influence on American intellectual, cultural, and political life than this one."[58]

The Pilgrims and the Puritans who came to this country in the early 1600s were God-fearing individuals who sought religious freedom and wanted to establish a country that would advance the

126

Christian faith. Those first settlers believed it was the parents' responsibility to educate their children. They came for freedom from church and governmental oppression and did not want the government to have the responsibility of seeing that their children learned to read and write. The fact that there is nothing specifically stated in the US Constitution about education indicates that those who were the early arrivals felt that education was not the government's responsibility.

Using the Bible as a textbook they educated children to be lovers of God, obedient to their parents, and to love their new country. Today we have no Bible in the classroom. The students in some classrooms are unmanageable and disobedient. Our children believe that every religion is equally the same, and that our country is guilty of gross injustice because of our affluence. We have indeed come a long way from the original intent of our Founding Fathers. We cannot produce moral, patriotic individuals without a biblical foundation.

In 2004, the late Father John Neuhaus, one of the leading spiritual intellectuals of our day, spoke to a group in New York City at a gathering called "Socrates in the City." Father Neuhaus addressed the question, "Can an atheist be a good citizen?" At the conclusion of a well thought out speech, Father Neuhaus said, "I reluctantly conclude, atheists cannot be good citizens. Thank you."[59] His reason was that a Christian"s allegiance is not to a regime or its body of works but to a God who is the Creator of heaven and earth and who calls men and women to be accountable to His law above all the laws and texts of man. In other words, we are to be morally accountable to what Neuhaus calls *a higher order.*

Prayer of Repentance for Allowing Christian Schools to Be Taken Over by Humanists

Father, in the Name of Jesus, I come to You. First of all, I repent for allowing humanists to take over our schools and in particular our colleges and universities. I ask forgiveness for our educational system for following after other gods and abandoning You and Your spiritual principles. Forgive us for our pride in assuming that intellect is the supreme measure of a man and in the development of the intellect man assumes that he knows more than You.

I pray that Your Word will be preached on every college and university campus, not with words of human wisdom, but with power and with a demonstration of the Spirit of God.

I bind a spirit of pride that exalts itself against the living God. I bind a spirit of idolatry that causes the mind of man to seek after the reasoning of the world and go toward ungodliness.

I bind the spirit of pride that deceives men and women and exalts the mind of man above God. In place of pride will be a spirit of humility and meekness that will fill every heart on every campus.

I lift up a standard that every institution of higher learning will be filled with the knowledge of God as the waters cover the sea.

I ask that the Spirit of wisdom and revelation be released in every college and university in the United States and every satellite institution in the world.

Father, I ask You to fill positions with men and women who will not only teach their subject matter but who will also be led by the Spirit of God. May Jesus be lifted up in the classrooms across America. May Jesus show Himself strong to everyone in our schools. (2 Corinthians 4:4.) Open the eyes of the unbelievers so the truth can be revealed. I pray this in the mighty Name of Jesus, the Name that is above every name. (Philippians 2:9.) Amen.

Read the Baal Divorce Decree and Divorce the spirit of Baal over the college or university.

Prophetic Declarations

Heavenly Father, through the power of the blood of Christ, by the Spirit of Truth and Grace, by the authority vested in me as a believer, and through the finished work of the Cross, I legislate, command, and declare:

1. (insert name of school) may have forsaken You, but it will return and become a fountain of living water. (Jeremiah 2:13.)

2. Jesus, You told us to ask You for laborers to go into the harvest, so we ask that You send Godly men and women to (insert name of school) to work here. Send professors, students, chaplains, administrators, board members, and students, who know You and who will proclaim Your Name at (insert name of school) and who will lift up a standard of righteousness. (Matthew 9:38.)

3. I thank God for (insert name of school) because of His grace given them in Christ Jesus. For in Him this school has been enriched in every way—in all speaking and knowledge. (1 Corinthians 1:4–5.)

4. I declare that there will be a demonstration of the Spirit's power at (insert name of school), so that its faith might not rest on men's wisdom, but on God's power. (1 Corinthians 2:4–5.)

5. The ungodly will not flourish here. (Psalm 1:4–6.)

6. Jesus, I declare that Your light and Your truth will guide all those at (insert name of school), Your light will bring them to You and to the place where You dwell. (Psalm 43:3.)

7. I lift up the Name of Jesus over (insert name of school). Your Word says that if His Name is lifted up, He will draw all men to Himself. (John 12:32.)

8. The foolishness of God is wiser than man's wisdom and the weakness of God is stronger than man's strength; therefore, I declare that the wisdom of Jesus has come to (insert name of

school) and He will be to you righteousness, holiness, and redemption. (1 Corinthians 1:25.)

9. My purpose is that all those at (insert name of school) may be encouraged in heart and united in love, so that they may have the full riches of complete understanding, in order that (insert name of school) may know the mystery of God, namely, Christ, in whom are hidden all the treasures of wisdom and knowledge. (Colossians 2:2–3.)

10. I declare that the God of our Lord Jesus Christ, the glorious Father, may give to (insert name of school) the Spirit of wisdom and revelation so that (insert name of school) may know Him better. I pray also that the eyes of every person's heart may be enlightened in order that they may know the hope to which He has called them, the riches of His glorious inheritance in the saints, and His incomparably great power for those who believe. That power is like the working of His mighty strength, which He exerted in Christ when He raised Him from the dead and seated him at His right hand in the heavenly realms, far above all rule and authority, power and dominion, and every title that can be given, not only in the present age but also in the one to come. And God placed all things under His feet and appointed Him to be head over everything for the church, which is His body, the fullness of Him who fills everything in every way. (Ephesians 1:17–23.)

Physical Place of Repentance

Location for National Repentance:

The major place for repentance for the United States is at Harvard University, located in Cambridge, Massachusetts.

Location for Local Repentance:

At the state level, I suggest that research be done on local universities that were founded by churches and then taken over by the government or by others with a humanistic agenda. It is astounding how many of our local universities with Godly foundations have succumbed to doctrines of humanism.

30 Entry Point # 2: Public School Education

Today almost every neighborhood in America has a public school. They are accessible and free. We take them for granted and many assume that public schools were instituted from the inception of America. But public schools funded by the government were not always a part of our society. In the beginning, when we were a commonwealth consisting of colonies, churches, and local communities, parents took responsibility for the education of children by establishing what were known as *common schools*, financed by land grants along with contributions from the local communities.

These schools were established to teach children to study the Bible and to prepare them to enter universities like Harvard where they would learn to become clergymen and magistrates. Under this system of local schools directly influenced by the church, America was undoubtedly the most literate society in the world. It may well be that the institution of free non-religious education is one of the single most important factors in the downward slide of education in American schools today.

Because of newly enlightened ideas that were blowing across the ocean, by 1818 there were many who saw the church as too confining, with too much influence over the students. They wanted education apart from religion. After all, Prussia (the German empire that was officially dismantled in 1947) had used public schools very well to indoctrinate the young minds of its constituents in the political and social agenda of the leaders. Why not use the same tactic in America, provide it for free, and require mandatory attendance?

Progressive educators and politicians insisted that the government create public primary schools like those in Prussia. Because the parochial schools were so successful, the public had to be persuaded to finance and enroll their children in a school with a secular and political objectives. A survey was taken in the city of Boston and the data collected revealed that a small percentage of poor children were not attending any school. Although the percentage was less than 10 percent, that was of no consequence. It was enough to take to the Massachusetts congress and request that allocation be made for the establishment of public schools separate from parochial schools for these poor children.

Government could have subsidized already existing church schools and thereby utilize the buildings, teachers, and educational structure already in place, but it chose not do so because these church schools were staffed with educators and clergy who taught children about God.

Those who felt the need to provide public schooling apart from churches did so because they wanted children to be exposed to ideas other than those expressed by the church. So the problem was never one of economics; it was, from the very beginning, philosophical. It was a clash of two world views—the socialists (secularists) against the Christians. This is a battle that continues until this day. Socialists push a social agenda on our children in public schools devoid of any moral compass and blame Christians for holding back the tide of progress when any complaint is voiced.

Enter Horace Mann, the politician responsible for convincing the Massachusetts state legislature to fund the public schools. Today Mann is revered in textbooks on the history of education as **"The Father of Public Education."** Every teacher who has graduated with a degree in education has heard of Horace Mann and the wonderful work he did in establishing public education for children. Without viewing his work and efforts from a biblical perspective, it's easy to think of him as a hero. After all, he made public education available to poor children. What could be wrong with that?

Without taking into consideration that the Christian churches and Christian schools in the day were already doing an excellent job of educating children, Mann, a Unitarian, wanted education free from the confines of religion and as a fulfillment of a campaign promise to liberal constituents and educators, he was able to pass legislation to set up a government public school system with as little religious teaching as possible.

Because most of the people in the state of Massachusetts were Christians and wanted at least some religious education, even in public schools, and had no interest in their children being taught socialism, ridding the schools of all Christian teaching would be virtually impossible. Mann realized that the process for setting up Christianity-free schools would require a more long-term strategy. Mann and the liberal Unitarians considered themselves the educated elite of the day and the Christians less sophisticated so they began the process of forming organizations that would foster more progressive-thinking among the people. They had literally become the wisdom of this world that Paul mentions in 1 Corinthians 1:19 where he states, "I will destroy the wisdom of the wise; the intelligence of the intelligent I will frustrate."

Progressives soon learned that in order to change America they would have to first change the educational system from the top down. Finding resistance with parents and teachers, they came to the second realization: that they would first have to set up teachers' colleges financed by the government that would train teachers in a secular curriculum. Most of the colleges at that time were Christian colleges and teachers were educated in the Bible as well as in their teaching discipline.

Once they had a biblical background, teachers were difficult to persuade to teach a secular agenda. Perhaps they saw the effectiveness of biblical teaching and didn't want to change. Mann and his cohorts devised the plan to establish what would become known as *Normal Schools* where teachers would be trained in a secular world view. This was an experiment in education contrary to the thought of the majority of people in that day, which is true of most public educational policies that have been implemented throughout our history. The secularists, in order to achieve their goals, have circumvented the wishes of the general public and have implemented their ideas through national organizations like the NEA and presently the National Department of Education.

Each state received land grant money to establish normal schools. So not only did Horace Mann set up public schools, he positioned them in such a way that they would be staffed by some of the brightest minds trained in ivy league colleges that would promote his doctrine. He knew it would take time, but eventually his plan would succeed.

One college textbook pictures Mann as a radical dreamer and social reformer, whose radical ideas, especially about property ownership, would make America a better place. Mann felt that property was to be viewed as leased from God and not owned. It was a rather unpopular thought among the independent Americans who had fled Europe to come to America where they could own their own land. Mann's appeal was to the working class and that is where he went to get support for his common school movement.

Secular educators believed that common schools that used a secular curriculum would promote a society that was devoid of class or race. They felt that the better educated person was, the more moral he would become. Mann and secularists like him were wrong, for it is only when a man knows Jesus that he will neither sees a man's standing in society nor his race.

With obvious distain for Christians, especially in the public arena, Mann fought with Christians frequently, especially the schoolmasters in Boston. Mann wanted to limit their influence over the lives of children. In 1845, as Secretary of the newly created Massachusetts Board of Education, Mann delivered to the public what he had promised—the first state normal school. This was a state-financed and state-controlled teachers' college. His second normal school was financed in part by the help of a prominent Unitarian along with matching funds from the state of Massachusetts.[60]

In 1845, Horace Mann delivered a speech at the dedication of his new normal schools where he renamed the new schools as **State Normal Schools**. However difficult the task was, Mann won the battle and Normal Schools would eventually crop up all across the nation as teachers colleges. Financed by government funding they would be the channel to feed our nation's children secular education apart from an education based on the Bible. What Mann realized, along with others who followed enlightened European teachers of the day, is that a country's educational system is the backbone of a country. Once the minds of one generation are captured, the evolution process of secularization of a country gets easier with each generation.

One textbook on the history of American education states:
"The common school movement unleashed a set of ideas and a series of trends that are still in motion... They should foster morality and ethics but avoid sectarian entanglements...The degree to which these and other objectives could be met through a system of schools more uniform in support, control, access, and ideology was problematic at best in the nineteenth century."[61]

A contemporary influencer of Horace Mann who is worth noting was a Scotsman by the name of Robert Owen. Today, he is known as the father of socialism. He was a wealthy manufacturer from Scotland who had been enlightened to the fact that man is a product of his society and not of his parents or his God. Owen published his views in 1813–1816. He believed the earlier society could begin to educate a child the better off that child would be for society.

Owen is responsible for the idea that education should be established for the good of society where a child would be brought up to think more in line with the wishes of the society that trained him or her. Owen also believed the only way to truly educate a child for society's good was to first educate the teachers to think in line with the new socialistic views. He advocated and was able to strongly influence Mann in the starting of teachers colleges, whereby teachers could be controlled by those whom he thought had society's best interest at heart. Owens' ideas were carried out by Horace Mann.

In his book, ***NEA: Trojan Horse in American Education***, Samuel Blumenfeld says about Horace Mann:

"If any single person can claim credit for changing American social, academic, and ultimately political direction from libertarian to a statist one, the credit must go to Horace Mann, for it was Mann who was able to overcome the considerable opposition to statism, while others could not. The key to Mann's success was in his peculiar sense of mission, combined with his practical political experience as a legislator, and the strong financial, cultural, and social backing of the Harvard Unitarian elite."[62]

Mr. Blumenfeld's uses the word "statism" to refer to the government. Americans in Horace Mann's day were rugged individualists who wanted very little government intervention in their lives. For Mann to convenience parents to let the state provide an education for their children was a major accomplishment. Once that was accomplished, the stage was set for the government to have ultimate control over the education of America's children.

What Happened in the Realm of the Spirit?

With the establishment of schools apart from Christian influence and with the establishment of non-Christian teacher training schools that would provide teachers for those schools, the stage was set to separate this country from its Christian roots. The battle for the minds of the nation would be won. It would take 100 years, but the course was a sure route to humanism. Our forefathers had come to the shores of America for a new life, one that included freedom of religion, yet the battle for the mind that had started in the Garden of Eden when Eve ate the fruit from the tree of the knowledge of good and evil proved to be an ongoing war that had to be fought many times over the course of history. (Genesis 3.) It was a war in which Christians would never be able to let down their guard, for when they did, the vacuum quickly filled with a godless philosophy that exalted man above the living God.

Prayer of Repentance for Public Education Separated from Christian Education

Father, I pray this prayer in the Name of Jesus. First of all, I repent for myself, my ancestors, and my generation for permitting the schools in this nation to allow only secular instruction. Forgive our nation for not teaching our children about You and Your ways. I repent for the sins of our forefathers, as allowed decisions to be made that allowed humanism into our schools. I repent for the sin of believing that man is god and is in no need of a Savior. Forgive Christians for disengaging in our educational system. From this day forward, bring Godly leaders who will take a bold stand for You in every facet of education. I ask for forgiveness for allowing a perverse spirit, which permeated the Age of Enlightenment, to influence the thinking, actions, and reasoning of my generation. Forgive Americans for believing that all religions and spiritual belief systems are equal. Forgive Americans for believing that having no religion in schools is better than allowing Christianity in schools. Forgive Americans for not teaching Your ways to our children and our children's children.

Jesus, I pray for a reformation in our educational system. Let there be a righteous indignation among the people of this nation, especially among the Christians who have their children in public schools, to bring about change in our schools. Let those parents and children stand strong and say, "We will no longer serve the god of the world, but we will serve the living God who will deliver us from the hands of the ungodly." I speak life into Christians across this nation. Let Godly people take their place of authority in the realm of the Spirit and turn back the tide of ungodly teaching contrary to sound biblical teachings in our schools.

Father, heal us of our hardness of heart. Soften the hearts of the people in America to be receptive to Your Word.

Let us realize that we are not more intelligent than You. You are the source of Wisdom and I ask You to be the wisdom and knowledge that our students need. Let the fear of God spread throughout our educational system so our students can know wisdom.

As a nation of educators, we have traded the truth for a lie. Forgive us and make Your truth known to every student, teacher, administrator, and support staff. Raise up intercessors across this land who will seek Your face on behalf of our educational system and all the children involved in every school in America. Let us see Your resurrection power in every child and then in every school.

I realize that my battle is not against principalities, rulers, and authorities of this age but is in the unseen realm, which is influencing people and leading them astray and into captivity. Thank You for a reformation in our schools across America. I pray this in Jesus Name. Amen.

Prophetic Declarations

Heavenly Father, through the power of the blood of Christ, by the Spirit of Truth and Grace, by the authority vested in me as a believer, and through the finished work of the Cross, I legislate, command, and declare:

1. The children in our schools will know the truth and the truth will set them free. (John 8:32.)

2. I count the American educational system to be dead to sin and alive to God in Christ Jesus. Sin will not reign over our schools, students, teachers, and administrators. They will not obey sin and its evil desires. (Romans 6:11–12.)

3. Bless those who are not offended because of You. (Matthew 11:6.)

4. There will be a demonstration of the Spirit and power of God. The faith of our children, teachers, and parents will not rest on men's wisdom, but on God's power. (1 Corinthians 2:4–5.)

5. The light of the Gospel of Jesus Christ will be manifest through every school in America. (John 1:5.)

6. I stand at the crossroads and look; I ask for the ancient paths of our forefathers in their original intent for the education of the children of this nation. (Jeremiah 6:16.)

7. I make the declaration that the prophet Elijah did when he confronted the prophets of Baal. You will let it be known today that You are God in Israel and that I am Your servant. Answer me, O Lord, answer me, so these people will know that You, O Lord, are God and that You are turning their hearts back again. (1 Kings 18: 36–37.)

8. Today I declare that as You have set before us life and death, blessings and curses, I choose life, so that I and the children of this nation may live. Every child in our educational system will love the Lord our God, listen to His voice, and hold fast to Him. For the Lord is their life and He will give them many years in this land. (Deuteronomy 30:19–20.)

9. I declare that the Name of our God will be remembered from generation to generation. (Exodus 3:15.)

10. I declare that no one will lead the children of America astray. Just as the Son of God came to destroy the works of the devil, we say that that work of unrighteous teaching in our schools is destroyed. (1 John 3:7–8.)

PHYSICAL PLACE OF REPENTANCE

Location for National Repentance:

The primary location for repentance is at the Statue of Horace Mann located in front of the Massachusetts State Senate, Boston, Massachusetts.

Location for Local Repentance:

Every state has a State Board of Education located either at the state capital building or nearby. Horace Mann made his promise to the state of Massachusetts to create secular public schools as a campaign promise in his bid as the first secretary of the newly created Massachusetts Board of Education.

Also each state has universities that were once normal schools that were created to teach a humanistic doctrine to teachers who would then teach in rural areas in America. A quick Internet search by state will give the list of normal schools in each state. The names of these schools have changed from the point of their creation, but they are still relatively easy to locate.

31 Entry Point # 3 Education of Children Given to the State

Acommon parental response to a teacher asking for a parent's help to address a child's misconduct in the classroom is, "it's your problem. You take care of it."

Those of us over the age of 50, remember our parents telling us that if we got in trouble in the classroom we would be deeper trouble once we got home. Times have changed and so has the attitude of many parents. Their plates are full as they juggle multiple jobs, absentee fathers and mothers, out-of-control children as well as multiple activities per child that must have equal attention as the classroom.

Today the school is no longer an extension of the family but rather the attitude is that the school is expected to take care of a child apart from the home. Where did the idea start that the government, or state, would be responsible to educate a child and the parent would have no say in his or her child's curriculum, nor would the parent support classroom discipline? As with many other entry points the decision to relinquish the education of our children to the government/state started at the turn of the century.

The first notice we have of the idea was in 1898 when the Kansas Teachers' Union prepared a book to commemorate Christopher Columbus Day. In this landmark book, the teachers gave credence to the two methods of education: secular education and religious education. A choice had to be made: was education to be administered by the religious schools of the day or was it to be administered by the state? Some leading educational historians, like Samuel Blumenfeld, believed that the Kansas Teachers' Union gave all authority to the state to educate children in Kansas. Others, like David Barton, believed that the Columbus Day book gave the option to a parent to give religious education or secular education to their children. Either way, the declaration made clear that there were two different views on how children should be educated.

The section in question states:

"Whether this [decision] was wise or not is not [our] purpose to discuss further than to remark, that if the study of the Bible is to be excluded from all state schools, if the inculcation of the principles of Christianity is to have no place in the daily program, if the worship of God is to form no part of the general exercises of these public elementary schools, then the good of the state would be better served by restoring all schools to church control."[63]

The Kansas Teachers' Union stated that schools should be one or the other—either secular or religious—but not try to be both. If the state was to educate children, then the state education should be secular. If the churches were to educate the children, then the education should be religious. The intent was to make a clear delineation between the two worldviews and grant permission to the state to take control of the education including teachers, teacher education, and curriculum, and make them secular and devoid of any Christian influence.

One of the main pillars of socialism is education of children by the government and the earlier the better. Socialists, or Progressives as they are called in the United States because they believe that man is morally progressing to a better state of human goodness, contend that controlling education is the way to assure that this human goodness will continue into the future.

It was German philosopher Georg Friedrich Hegel (1770–1831) who promoted the idea that man was the highest manifestation of God in the universe, thereby elevating man to godlike status and if trained in the right manner, man would dispense justice and equality above what was taught in the Scriptures. Many educators studied under Hegel in Germany and brought his ideas back to the US to implement in our educational system.

Educational elite, like John Dewey, also traveled to Russia to glean the ideas that they felt made the Russian educational system successful. Enamored with the Communist-run schools that promoted early education, national support, centralized control, and upheld rigorous mandatory attendance, Dewey wanted the same for America.

To the unspiritual, educated mind the idea of using education to further secular progress was doable and realistic. Dewey sincerely felt his new methods would improve learning and was elated at their acceptance by the educated elite.

Adolf Hitler said in 1933, "When an opponent declares, 'I will not come over to your side,' I calmly say, "Your child belongs to us already. What are you? You will pass on. Your descendants, however, now stand in the new camp. In a short time, they will know nothing else but this new community."[64]

The Progressives want our children for their own agenda and that agenda from the very onset was to do away with Christian teaching of any kind in our public schools. If Christians teach moral restraint, free markets and individualism, the Progressives would never achieve their goal of creating a socialized collective society. Their patience won out and with the slow drip of secular, state-induced teaching, secularists have taken our schools down a path that only intercessors will be able to reverse!

On a front that is just as serious, the UN is at our heels wanting to assert its authority over the education of our children. At this point, not only do we need to be concerned with the educational mandates the US government implements through the legislative and judicial branches of our government, we must also look behind our backs at the United Nations' endeavors. In the mid 1990s, the UN proposed a treaty known as the Convention on the Rights of the Child (**UNCRC**). Meant to protect the rights of every child in the world below the age of 18 (unless a country had a law in place that stated the legal age less than 18), the treaty addresses child custody and guardianship laws.

Some of the rights of the child that are included is the right to life, the right to a name and identity, the right to be raised by his parents and a right to have a relationship with both parents even if the parents are separated. Capital punishment as well as cruel and degrading punishment is forbidden. The treaty states that parents have the primary responsibility for their children. However, the government would be the one to determine what was ultimately in the best interest of the child. Parental control and authority would be undermined. Madeline Albright, the presiding ambassador from the United States to the United Nations, signed the treaty in 1995, but it was never ratified by the US Senate.

The Convention on the Rights of the Child was ratified by every government in the world with the exception of Somalia, South Sudan, and the United States. Somalia indicated that it would ratify the treaty later. The major block of opposition to the treaty came from conservatives and more specifically from the Heritage Foundation and the powerful home schooling lobby, the Homeschool Legal Defense Association (**HSLDA**). President Barack Obama described the failure of the US to ratify the Convention as embarrassing and promised to review the process to see if the treaty could be ratified at a later date.

Thank God for those who, like the Heritage Foundation and the Homeschooling Lobby, watch at our gates to prevent policies, laws, judgments, and treaties that would undermine the right of parents to have control over their own children.

What Happened in the Spirit Realm?

When God called Abram to leave his homeland in the Ur of the Chaldeans and go with his family to a new land called Canaan, He was asking Abram to completely break away from his traditions and the security he had in his father's house. God wanted a family with whom He could make covenant. His promise to Abram is found in Genesis 12:2–3, "I will make you into a great nation and I will bless you; I will make your Name great, and you will be a blessing. I will bless those who bless you, and whoever curses you I will curse; and all peoples on earth will be blessed through you." There was a purpose for Abram's separation from the world and that was for Abram to serve the one true God and raise his descendents to do the same.

When we separate our children apart from the world and submit them to teaching about the one true God, the Creator of heaven and earth, then we position our seed to receive a blessing from God and to become a blessing to all the other families in the earth. To subject our children to secular teaching where they sit under godless curriculum often administered by godless persons, removes them from the line of God's blessings.

When our country was first formed, the majority of our teachers were those who loved God and worshiped Him alone. It was only at the beginning of the twentieth century that public schools began the severing process to eliminate all religious teaching. It didn't happen in a short time frame.

It would take us one hundred years to come to this place and many parents who were raised attending public schools still may remember that their teachers were Godly men and women who endeavored to teach within a moral Christian framework. It would be nice if this was the case today, but it isn't. Today even if a teacher believes in God, he or she has been muzzled by the court system of this land, and can proclaim nothing about a loving God who cares about all children as individuals and holds each person accountable for his sins.

The writing of secular curricula that did not recognize God and the training of teachers in secularism were the two main prongs used to make our schools more secular. Once our children were not taught about God, they were removed from the line of blessings that God promised Abram. Just as we don't wake up one day and know all about God, neither do our children learn about God in a day. It takes daily devotion to instructing, not just our children, but also ourselves in the ways of God for someone to have a comprehension of His nature.

Daily classroom instruction and positive reference to God, reinforced by what is taught in the family, culminate in producing a moral person who loves God. Parents who have their children in public schools have a greater responsibility to fill in the spiritual void left by the school. Christian schools coupled with parental reinforcement can do an excellent job as well as those Christian parents who homeschool their children.

Prayer of Repentance for Relinquishing the Education of Our Children to the State

Father, I ask in the Name of Jesus for the educational systems already in place in each state to be opened up to teach about the one true and living God, the Creator of heaven and earth, the Father of our Lord Jesus Christ who will be exalted in our classrooms and in our families.

I pray for Your forgiveness for relinquishing our rights as parents that allowed the government to take over the responsibility to educate our children. Raise up strong mothers and fathers who will instruct their children in learning about You. Let   parents once again take responsibility to teach and instruct their children in the knowledge of God. I repent for our forefathers who relinquished the education of their children to the state.

I pray You release the unholy bond on Christian teachers, administrators, and board members so they can freely be conveyers of Your spiritual knowledge to their students.

Lord, You see that the leaders have conspired against You in our educational system. I ask that You consider their threats and enable those who are called by Your Name to speak Your word with great boldness. Stretch out Your hand to heal and perform miraculous signs and wonders through the Name of Your holy servant Jesus. Amen.

Prophetic Declarations

1. I declare that the children in this nation will love the Lord their God with all their heart and with all their souls and with all their minds. They will love their neighbors as themselves. (Matthew 22:37–39.)

2. You, O God, make America a great nation. You bless every school in this nation. You bless those who bless us and whoever curses us, You will curse. Through America all the peoples of the earth will be blessed. The Godly seed of this nation is blessed and through them all the nations of the earth will be blessed. (Geneses 12:2-3.)

3. Mothers and fathers will arise to teach their children in the way of righteousness. (Deuteronomy 4:9.)

4. In every school, classroom, teacher, and student in this country, You create a hunger and thirst for righteousness. (Matthew 5:6.)

5. I lift up the Name of Jesus over every school in America and believe Your Word when Jesus said, "I, when I am lifted up from the earth, will draw all men to myself." (John 12:32.)

6. I declare that signs and wonders will be performed in every classroom in America. You will show Yourself strong on behalf of those who call on the Name of Jesus. (Proverbs 18:10.)

7. Every school in America will know the truth and the truth will set them free. (John 8: 32.)

8. The children of our nation are trained in the way they should go and when they are old they will not depart from it. (Proverbs 22:6.)

9. You give the children a heart for You so they will not be stubborn and rebellious, but they will be those whose hearts are loyal to God. (Psalm 78:5–8.)

10. Even though our children may have been taught in the ways of the world they will embrace Your truth. (Acts 7:22.)

PHYSICAL PLACE OF REPENTANCE

Location for the National Repentance:

Kansas State Department of Education
120 SE 10th Ave.
Topeka, Ks

Location for Local Repentance:

Pray at your state Department of Education building or choose any local school and pray at that location.

32 Entry Point # 4: Humanist Manifesto

From the very beginning of the battle for secularization of our schools, the enemy was humanism. John Dewey is the one who gave the movement a name and nourished the fledgling effort until it was full blown in our educational system. John Dewey created a network of institutions and highly influential individuals who would implement his concepts, proposals, and theories out to the far reaches of this country. Humanism is now a major stronghold with roots in idol worship.

Among liberal educators, John Dewey is heralded as a hero. His prolific writings in the late 1800s and early 1900s on socialism and education revolutionized America's traditional schools. Public schools at the turn of the century emphasized a rugged individualism that was characteristic of our Founding Fathers. He was called a social Progressive who wanted to educate our children into a collective society that would emerge in the twenty-first century. Dewey believed that just as man physically evolved from animals, man also evolved socially. The evolution process occurred according to man's ability to adjust to the social events in his world. Because of this evolution, a child should be educated to become a social citizen.

With a socialist agenda, Dewey wanted collective thinkers. Children who were individualistic and who could not conform to his ideas of social living did not fit in this new world order. They would not be prepared for the new social order Dewey hoped would evolve in America.

At the time, Dewey presented his innovative ideas in his book *The New Republic*, which was largely dismissed by the public because of his outlandish new theories. However, Dewey was patient and now more than one hundred years later we see the effect of his theories on every public and most private schools in our country. According to Dewey, the classroom emphasis should be on cooperative activity with little room for student autonomy. Dewey sought to create a mindset among the children so they would function in a group setting, leaving no room for individualism.

In 1899, Dewey wrote *School and Society*, which was an instant hit with the Progressives and shaped much of the social content of the new curriculum the social progressive educators of the day were demanding. Dewey's ideas converged with several other streams of Progressive thought for a maximum impact on our schools. Dewey initially presented two new streams of thought: (1) The new study discipline of behavioral psychology that was emerging as a new science and promoted teaching methods of training children in the same manner one would train animals; (2) evolution was the science of the day and children should be taught the facts of this new science.

According to Dewey all vestiges of Christianity were outdated and needed to be removed from the curriculum. All references to God or traditional values were to be viewed as obstacles to social progress.

In the implementation of Dewey's program, man was set as the standard of his own learning. Man was god. Learning was supreme. There would be no need of man to depend on a creator or a savior. The new curriculum that came from Dewey's theories was designed to create a new democratic socialist citizen capable of leading the way into the twentieth century.

One look inside a contemporary elementary school classroom today will reveal John Dewey's successful fingerprint. Desks clustered together and learning centers that promote a collective learning approach. Dewey succeeded in his vision. In large numbers, our students have been taught to accept and revere every religious group on equal footing. Christianity is no longer honored as being better than Hinduism, Buddhism, Judaism, Islam, or Wiccan. Christianity is, after all, an imperialist's religion less acceptable than the others because, according to the prevailing thought, Christians have had the upper hand far too long.

Harvard Progressives put Dewey's ideas into their curriculum and began the process of forever changing education. It was the trickle-down effect that jump-started our schools on the road to socialism. It is interesting to note that John Dewey, the renowned socialist educator who served the NEA in various capacities, near the end of his life, was given an honorary membership in that organization.

In 1933, John Dewey met with thirty-three other liberal Progressives and drew up and signed an extraordinary document known as the *Humanist Manifesto*. This Manifesto is a benchmark event in the turning of our schools away from God for it directly states the opposition the new order had against God.

"The time has come for widespread recognition of the radical changes in religious beliefs throughout the modern world….In order that religious humanism may be better understood we, the undersigned, desire to make certain affirmations which we believe the facts of our contemporary life demonstrate. There is great danger of a final, and we believe fatal, identification of the word religion with doctrines and methods which have lost their significance and which are powerless to solve the problem of human beings living in the Twentieth Century."[65]

The Manifesto held to certain tenets, among them: the belief that the universe is self-existing and not created; man has no soul;

traditional religion is to be rejected; man is to tend the environment of the planet; religion consists of actions, purposes, and experiences that are humanly significant. As for the purpose of life, the humanist's belief, stated in the Manifesto, is, "Religious humanism considers the complete realization of human personality to be the end of man's life and seeks its development and fulfillment in the here and now. This is the explanation of the humanist's social passion."[66]

Secular Humanism

How did our classrooms become a battleground for the minds of our children? Why are we at the point where children can kill children in the classrooms? When a school killing occurs, fear raises it's ugly head and more than one spiritual battle must be fought. I have seen students in Oklahoma become fearful because a school shooting occurred in Arkansas. As intercessors, we are not only called on to believe God for death to be dispelled from the classroom, but also to deal with the fear that occurs when tragedy strikes.

How did we get from a Godly system to a godless one? There are numerous entry points that I discuss in subsequent chapters, the major undercurrent of all of the Historical Entry Points is Secular Humanism. The belief that man is basically good and only needs to be educated to me a moral person has undermined our educational system. This belief that we do not need God shows up in the curriculum of almost every subject. It is taught in our colleges to future teachers. It is the belief of the National Education Association.

The battle in which we are engaged is for the lives of our children, and is spiritual warfare and can only be won on a spiritual level. Christians must realize that the battle will only be won when we learn to take a stand in the spirit realm and refuse to let the lies of the devil convert our youth to where they readily obey the forces of evil rather than the commandments of God.

We see more exploitation of children in the world today than at any other time in history. Even the United Nations, that supposedly is a bastion for civil rights, is now backpedaling on issues of child brides, human trafficking, honor killings, education, and child labor. These issues are now labeled as cultural and should not be touched. Just like King Herod issued an order that children two years old and under were to be killed, because he had received word that the Messiah had been born. Now Satan is out to kill this generation because each child has the potential for generating one of the greatest revivals in history in his generation. (Matthew 2:16.)

What Happened in the Realm of the Spirit?

With the Humanist Manifesto, public schools had a definition of the new materialist religion in which humanity sets itself up as god instead of the God who created this world and everything in it. The religion of Secular Humanism has become the official religion of the United States, for it is the only religion permitted in its public schools and totally supported by government funds.

It is possible to stand spiritually at this entry point and repent for the sins of our fathers for having believed a lie. After all, we, as sinners, repent for the sins of one man Adam because we all became partakers of that sin. Humanism has infected every facet of our life from the food we eat, to the television programs we watch, and to the clothes we wear.

In 1973, humanists reaffirmed their faith in secular humanism by issuing Humanist Manifesto II which says:

"As in 1933, humanists still believe that traditional theism, especially faith in the prayer-hearing God, assumed to love and care for persons, to hear and understand their prayers, and to be able to do something about them, is an unproved and outmoded faith. Salvationism, based on mere affirmation, still appears as harmful, diverting people with false hopes of heaven hereafter. Reasonable minds look to other means for survival... The next century can be and should be the humanistic century...."[67]

In 2003, the Humanist Manifesto III was written. Also known as "Humanism and Its Aspirations," the document once again affirms its belief in the good of man without God.

If we, as Christians, are to obtain victory over the demonic entry points of our educational system, we must contend with this false idiotic religion. It is Baal worship in it basic form. Humanism constitutes one of the greatest strongholds in our history.

Prayer of Repentance for Allowing Humanism in Our Schools

Father, I come to you in the Name of Jesus. I humble myself in repentance for allowing humanist teaching in our schools. This is an idol. There is no god but one, who is my Father, from whom all things came, whether in heaven or on earth. There is but one Lord, Jesus Christ, through whom we live. (1 Corinthians 8:4–13.)

Many educators and students are accustomed to the idol of humanism that they think nothing of teaching its principles; their conscious is weak and many are defiled so I ask that You reveal Yourself to them. Create in each one sensitivity to You and to Your Holy Spirit. Let them know You as Truth and Light.

Let us rise up tomorrow morning, just as Gideon did, to see the idol of humanism demolished along with all the vestiges of idol worship that John Dewey or any other Progressive brought into our schools. Let there be no defense left for humanism. Destroy its roots. We blow the trumpet of victory and send messengers throughout America to declare that humanism is dead. (Judges 6:27–5.)

Our students and educators are free to worship the one true God. We rejoice in the victory we have in Christ Jesus our Lord and Savior.

Prophetic Declarations

1. I declare that Mighty Warriors are being raised up who will confront and bring down the idolatrous practices of humanism. (Judges 6:12.)

2. I declare that the Lord Most High will demolish the altars of the wicked and will destroy their sacred foundations. (Hosea 10:2.)

3. I forget the former idols that were established in our schools and I will not dwell on their wickedness. You, O Lord, are doing a new thing. It springs up now. All will perceive it. You will make a way in the desert land of our educational system and You will build streams of living water in every classroom. You will give living water to Your people and they will proclaim Your praise. (Isaiah 43:18–21.)

4. Just as King Asa did what was right in the eyes of the Lord by expelling those who did abominable acts in the land and who worshiped idols. I expel those in our educational system who worship the idol of humanism. (1 Kings 15:11–15.)

5. Great is the Lord and most worthy of praise; He is to be feared above all gods. For the gods of the humanists are idols, but the Lord made the heavens. Splendor and majesty are before Him; strength and glory are in His sanctuary. (Psalm 96:4–6.)

6. I declare that all who are righteous and who tear down the altars of the idolatrous and feel as though they are the only one left, will have their eyes opened to see the multitudes who have not bowed their knee to Baal. (1 Kings 19:14–18.)

7. I declare that the students in our schools will not view knowledge as wisdom but will seek wisdom that comes from the one true God. (Genesis 3:6.)

8. I declare that the kingdom of American education has now become the kingdom of our Lord and of His Christ and He

will reign forever and ever. (Revelation 11:15.)

9. I declare that the weapons we fight with are not the weapons of the world. On the contrary, they have divine power to demolish strongholds. I demolish arguments and every pretension that sets itself up against the knowledge of God, and I take captive every thought to make it obedient to Christ. (2 Corinthians 10:4–5.)

10. Jesus said that when He was lifted up from the earth that He would draw all men unto Him. I declare that everyone in our entire educational system is drawn to Jesus. (John 12: 32.)

PHYSICAL PLACES FOR REPENTANCE

Location for National Repentance:

1. The University of Vermont is one of the primary places of repentance. When John Dewey died on June 1, 1952, he was buried on the north side of the Ira Allen Chapel on the University of Vermont campus in Burlington, Vermont. John Dewey was born October 20, 1859, in Burlington, Vermont and attended the University of Vermont.

2. The office of *The Humanist* magazine that first published the Manifesto at 1777 T St. NW, Washington, DC.

3. The New School in the Greenwich Village section of New York City, New York. The New School was founded by the four men who penned the first Humanist Manifesto and also houses the World Policy Institute.

Location for Local Repentance:

Almost every state in the US has a Humanist Organization that meets on a regular basis. Locate the meeting place and pray at that location. If you have a Unitarian Church in your area, that would be a good location to pray.

33 Entry Point #5: Prayer and Bible Reading Removed

In one of its 1964 issues, *Life* Magazine referred to Madalyn Murray O'Hair as "the most hated woman in America." Ms O'Hair, is often credited with filing the lawsuit that removed prayer from public schools. In 1963, her landmark Supreme Court case of *Murray v. Curlett*, the court rendered its decision that prayer in schools was unconstitutional. O'Hair's case was one of several that had come before the Supreme Court wanting prayer removed from the public classrooms. In each case, the Supreme Court ruled against not only lower court decisions but also the school districts who had wanted to retain the simple prayers that were allowed in classrooms and at public school-sponsored events. The result of the Supreme Court ruling was that Bible reading and prayer were removed from public schools.

It all started when O'Hair, an atheist, became angry when she heard her son's classroom was required to recite the Lord's Prayer at the beginning of class. O'Hair voiced a complaint complete with verbal expletives to the office personnel at the school and when she was ignored, she filed a lawsuit in the State of Maryland requesting that prayer and Bible reading be prohibited in public schools. O'Hair claimed that the board of education by requesting her son William to repeat the Lord's Prayer had violated the First and Fourteenth Amendments of the US Constitution. The Supreme Court of the State of Maryland ruled against O'Hair, but not one to take the loss lightly, she appealed her case to the Supreme Court of the United States, the highest court in the nation. This time she won. In the end, the highest court of our land rendered a decision that reversed the Maryland Court of Appeals decision to allow the Lord's Prayer and Bible reading in public schools. On June 17, 1963, the court announced that prayer and Bible reading in public school classrooms would no longer be constitutional. The court majority opinion said in part:

"The place of religion in our society is an exalted one achieved through a long tradition of reliance on the home, the church and the inviolable citadel of the individual heart and mind. We have come to recognize through bitter experience that it is not within the power of government to invade that citadel, whether its purpose or effect to aid or oppose, to advance or retard. In the relationship between man and religion, the state is firmly committed to a position of neutrality. The breach of neutrality that is today a trickling stream may all too soon become a raging torrent, and in the words of Madison, "It is proper to take alarm at the first amendment on our Liberties."[68]

The Supreme Court in an eight-to-one vote reversed the Maryland Court of Appeals decision and ruled that opening Bible reading and prayer exercises were unconstitutional not only in Maryland but also in the United States.

On the heels of the Murray O'Hair Supreme Court case that removed prayer and Bible reading from public schools came an equally impacting decision that reinforced the removal of prayer from our classrooms. The landmark lawsuit presented in 1962 was *Engel v. Vitale*. The offending prayer was known as the "Regents' Prayer," and stated, "Almighty God, we acknowledge our dependence upon

Thee, and we beg Thy blessings upon us, our parents, our teachers, and our country."

The prayer was recited with bowed heads and folded hands. The Board of Regents of the State of New York had prepared this simple prayer for use in New York's public schools. It was considered a part of the state's "Statement on Moral and Spiritual Training in the Schools." The regents took great pains to compose an invocation that would be both religiously and politically correct. The regents allowed exemption to any student who might be offended to be excused from the exercise.

Steven Engel escorted his son to Searingtown Elementary School one morning and watched him recite the Regents' Prayer along with the other students in the classroom. Engel took issue with the prayer and felt that it imposed a spiritual ritual contrary to the customs of his family's Jewish faith and traditions. Engel enlisted the help of nine other parents to file suit against the Long Island school board and its chairman.

The suit failed in the New York State Court of Appeals when the decision was handed down in favor of the school board. Engle and the others decided to take their appeal to the US Supreme Court. The Supreme Court weighed in on the side of the parents. It seems the Supreme Court was concerned that the government had no right to compose official prayers for any group of American people to recite. No official prayer would be carried on by any government institution.[69] Public opinion weighed in on the side of prayer. At the time, eighty-five percent of Americans favored prayer in schools. However, the axe had fallen and school-sponsored classroom prayers were out.

Even if a student never heard his or her teacher pray in a classroom, the fact that the US Justice System declared it illegal made a tremendous statement. The decision squelched any recognition of God through prayer and Bible references. Spiritual life in the classroom made an exit. Current data now reflects the negative effect elimination of prayer and Bible reading had on the morality of our students and on our classrooms. Since the early 1960s test scores have plummeted, teen pregnancy has skyrocketed, and school violence has escalated beyond our wildest imagination.

Throughout the next 25 years the Supreme Court would hear numerous cases that dealt with prayer in public schools. The case of *Engel v. Vitale* would be a benchmark for the Supreme Court as they would take great pains to protect the rights of the minority in areas of religious expression as they continued to prohibit any government-sponsored prayer from being invoked in the classroom. The court had interpreted the intentions of the Founding Fathers that government and religion should be separate and therefore no expression of the Christian religion was to be intertwined with public schools. The fact that our Founding Fathers didn't separate prayer from schools or for that matter any other part of life was not taken into consideration.

In 1964, there was a grass roots attempt to pass an amendment to the Constitution that would prohibit the Supreme Court from viewing cases dealing with school prayer. While many congressional members, such as Congressman Frank Becker from the Long Island district where the *Engel v. Vitale* case had originated, joined in on support for the amendment, some, such as Senator Birch Byah, chairman of the Senate Judiciary Subcommittee on Constitutional Amendments, were satisfied that the Supreme Court had ruled correctly.

Church leaders tried to put pressure on the Kennedy administration to support the amendment, but President Kennedy was unwilling to take up the cause and instead urged the American people to pray in their homes and to attend church more frequently. With all the push to get the amendment passed, it appeared that Congress would support the effort. However, the failure of the amendment lay in the lack of grass roots support for its passage. The American people voted by their indifference.[70]

The removal of prayer from the classroom was an issue that weighed heavily on the heart of President Ronald Regan as he advocated for freedom to restore nonsectarian prayers in a noncompulsory manner. President Reagan was hopeful when in 1985 the Supreme Court reviewed the case of *Wallace v. Jaffree*. This case challenged an Alabama statute that authorized teachers to conduct regular prayer in the classroom. At this time, public polls were 75 percent in favor of classroom prayer that would allow a one-minute period of meditation and prayer in public schools. The Supreme Court ruled against Alabama and once again did not allow prayer in classrooms. President Reagan was disappointed. The Alabama case was vague and many states found that allowing students to have a moment of silence would be okay with the courts as long as a teacher didn't tell the students to pray during that moment of silence.

What Happened in the Realm of the Spirit?

Once the Supreme Court rules on an issue, a new level of fear rises in the hearts and minds of believers, especially those in the public school classrooms. Along with the fear comes intimidation. Christian teachers who would never think of evangelizing in a public school classroom are intimidated and fearful of administrative and parental reprimands and refrain from all mention of Christianity in any form. Our classrooms moved to an extremely secular arena.

The very core of a Christian belief is in the existence of God and when that core belief is squelched the vacuum is filled with fear. With the Supreme Court rulings, a teacher who led her class in prayer or read the Bible was in danger of being arrested, losing her teaching position, having her teacher certification revoked, and even being taken to court in a civil suit. The Supreme Court added the teeth of the law to make sure no one dared implement two of the most basic Christian disciplines of prayer and Bible reading in a public classroom.

I was raised in the small town of Magnolia, Arkansas. The high school I attended had 450 students. I remember my teachers being outstandingly professional in every way. No one would have persecuted them in the late 1960s for praying in front of the students, mentioning Jesus, or reading the Bible in a classroom, but not one teacher did either of the three, at least not in my presence. They were schooled in separation of religion from public schools and they obeyed the rules. It might be well to note that if anyone on those teachers had been an atheist, they most likely wouldn't have been hired in the school system to begin with.

The scene was different when I first entered the classroom as a teacher twenty years later. I was continually reminded by my school administrators that I could not do certain things like read my Bible to the students, or quote Bible verses to them, nor could I speak with the students about Jesus. At this time in our school's history, the law required that teachers not engage in religious discussion or activities of any nature with the students. Even though I would have never evangelized my students, I was restrained from being who I was. This is the position in which most Christian teachers find themselves.

Our public education has seen a dramatic decline in test scores, morality, and family structure since the early 1960s, which is the same time that prayer and Bible reading were banned from the public school classroom. While these decisions were detrimental to our society, they were most likely the tipping point for our country that was already on a moral decline. These decisions pushed us over the precipice. We began to experience the first serious wave of socialism that John Dewey had implemented in the 1930s when he opted for a progressive and open classroom philosophy that would embrace all religions as equals.

Currently there are many parents, administrators, teachers, and students who would like to see prayer and Bible reading restored to the classroom. While it may be impossible to see how this could be accomplished, it can be done. It is not ours to tell God how to do it, but our position is one of faith to believe Him for the end result. It is what I call the "Fracking Principle." The many years I prayed with other intercessors for America to be energy independent, I never thought that God would come up with a new method of drilling. I had in my mind He would cause the US government to relax its ban on drilling on our own land and offshore. But God had new technology in mind and that may be what happens with education. It is the end result for which we have faith; it is not our job to tell Him how to get there.

Prayer of Repentance for Allowing Prayer and Bible Reading to Be Taken Out of Public Schools

Father, I come to You in the Name of Jesus. On behalf of believers in America, I ask Your forgiveness for allowing prayer and Bible reading, and ultimately You, to be taken out of our public schools and replaced with the idolatrous religion of secular humanism. Forgive us for our apathy and lack of political involvement. Forgive us for our lack of personal prayer and devotion to Jesus and to His Ways.

I stand in the gap on behalf of our nation and in particular our educational system. I ask that You not pour out your wrath on us, but rather that Your mercy and grace be upon America. (Ezekiel 22:30.).

You, O Lord, are the God of our Founding Fathers, and You rule over all the kingdoms and the nations. Power and might are in Your hand and no one, not even the Supreme Court of the United States, can withstand You. You brought believers to this nation who wanted to serve You in freedom. They lived here and built it as a sanctuary for You. Now look at the vast army of secularism that seeks to destroy us. See how secularism repays this nation for their freedom. They seek to drive us out of our schools and public places. For we have no power to face this vast army that is attacking us. I do not know what to do, but our eyes are upon You. Let Your people take up our positions and stand firm and see the deliverance the Lord will give us" (2 Chronicles 20:6–17). I pray this in the mighty Name of Jesus. Amen.

Prophetic Declarations

1. God did not give us a spirit of timidity (fear), but a spirit of power, of love and of self-discipline. (2 Timothy 1:7.)

2. I declare that the stone the builders rejected in our schools has become the cornerstone of education in America. Salvation is found in no one else but Jesus, for there is no other name under heaven given to men by which we must be saved. (Acts 4:11–12.)

3. I declare that it is better to obey God than man. Grant Your servants in the educational mountain of this great nation, boldness to speak Your Word so that signs and wonders will be done in the Name of Jesus. (Acts 4:19–20.)

4. Even though teachers, administrators, and students have been given strict orders not to teach in the Name of Jesus, I declare that Your teaching will fill every student, administrator, and teacher in our schools. (Acts 4:19–20.)

5. I declare that Your people are not ashamed of the gospel, because it is the power of God for the salvation of everyone who believes: first for the Jew, then for the Gentile. (Romans 1:16.)

6. I declare that every believer who remains in the public school system will be built up and not torn down. You, O God, will plant those who are righteous in our schools and You will uproot those who are not. You are grieved over the disaster that has come upon us. I will not be afraid of the rulers of this nation, who now bring fear in our classrooms. You are with us and will save and deliver us from the hands of those who mean evil against Your righteous ones. You will restore us to

the land of freedom in our schools. (Jeremiah 42:10–12.)

7. I declare that every classroom in America will be full of the knowledge of the Lord as the waters cover the sea. (Isaiah 11:9.)

8. I declare that the Lord will make Himself known in every classroom and people will acknowledge the Lord. They will worship Him and He will heal them. (Isaiah 19:21–22.)

9. I declare that the message of the Lord will spread rapidly and be honored. I declare that Your righteous ones will be delivered from wicked and evil men, for not everyone has faith. The Lord will be faithful. He will strengthen and protect every righteous one so they will continue in the faith. (2 Thessalonians 3: 1–5.)

10. I declare that the children in our schools obey the first and greatest commandment. They will love the Lord their God with all their hearts and with all their souls and with all their minds. (Matthew 22:37–38.)

PHYSICAL PLACE OF REPENTANCE

Location for National Repentance:

The United States Supreme Court
1 First Street, NE
Washington, DC 20543

Location for State Repentance:

Each state in the United States has a State Supreme Court. Locate the Supreme Court of your particular state and go there to repent.

30 Entry Point # 6: Ten Commandments Removed

In 1978, the state of Kentucky passed a law that required a copy of the Ten Commandments be posted in every public school classroom in the state. Funds for the plaques were to be purchased with private monies and would also have the following phrase on the same plaque, "The secular application of the Ten Commandments is clearly seen in its adoption as the fundamental legal code of Western civilization and the Common Law of the United States."

Two years later a lawsuit, *Stone v. Graham,* was filed with the Supreme Court of the United States to reverse the Kentucky law requiring the Ten Commandment postings. The Supreme Court of the United States ruled that posted copies of the Ten Commandments were unconstitutional and should be removed from the Kentucky classrooms, which made it clear that the same ruling would apply to every classroom in every state in the United States, should any other state think about requiring such postings.

The justification of the court ruling was that the posting of the Ten Commandments violated the Establishment Clause of the First Amendment, which states, "Congress shall make no law respecting an establishment of religion."

Although the copies were purchased with private funding, the fact that they were being placed in every public school classroom made the displays a violation of the First Amendment. So the Ten Commandments had to be removed.

The Ten Commandments are a reminder of America's spiritual heritage, which many would like to not only deny but wipe away altogether. When we see those who would rewrite our history, the one thing they continually want to omit is our Judeo-Christian foundation. George Santayana, a prominent philosopher, essayist, poet, and novelist said, "Those who cannot remember the past are condemned to repeat it." My contention is that if we rewrite history, then how can we remember it?

The first of the Ten Commandments says, "You shall have no other gods before me" (Exodus 20:3). That declaration is offensive to anyone who rejects the God that Jews and Christians worship, even if they contend that they worship God. Consider how many people are offended by Jesus, even though He healed sick people, opened blind eyes, and preached the Gospel to the poor, yet Jesus said, "Blessed is he, whosoever shall not be offended in me" (Luke 7:23 KJV).

Muldrow, Oklahoma is located in the eastern part of Oklahoma near Fort Smith, Arkansas in an area Oklahomans call Green Country, where rolling hills covered with lush green grass are dotted with cattle farms. With a population of less than 3,500 people, Muldrow is one of the least likely places to have a debate on the Ten Commandments. It seems that Muldrow's public school officials had plaques that contained copies of the Ten Commandments in their public school classrooms, clearly visible for all eyes and no one thought too much about it.

At some point in 2013, a student became offended that school authorities had the audacity to put the Ten Commandments in his classroom. The student sought for a way to remove the offending postings. He didn't have to look far to find an anti-God organization that would help him. He contacted the Freedom from Religion Foundation (FFRF), based in Madison, Wisconsin. FFRF then wrote a letter to the Muldrow Public School Superintendent requesting that he ensure that the numerous Ten Commandments postings be removed from the Muldrow Public Schools' classrooms. The letter from FFRF staff attorney Patrick Elliott, dated May 1, 2013, advised Muldrow superintendent Ron Flanagan that the display of the Ten Commandments constituted a *flagrant violation* of the Establishment Clause of the Constitution.

Many of the teachers, parents, and students were willing to fight to retain the plaques, but it was to no avail. The Muldrow School Board knew that the small town did not have the financial resources to fight FFRE's demands. All Ten Commandment postings were promptly removed from the classrooms, which pleased the FFRF. In a follow up response, FFRF co-president Annie Laurie Gaylor said:

> "We are pleased the school administration has removed the Ten Commandments, in compliance with the constitution. This is settled law. Public schools cannot advance or endorse religion. We hope the Board will 'Honor thy constitution,' and heed the advice of its attorney rather than to acquiesce to pressure from a religious mob."[71]

FFRF's request letter uses bullying terms like: "flagrant violation," "compliance with the constitution," "cannot advance or endorse religion," "honor thy constitution," and "religious mob." In reality, the Supreme Court is not as emphatic as Gaylor and the FFRF led the Muldrow school administration to believe. In the public school context, the Court held in *Stone v. Graham,* (1980) that the state could not require privately donated Ten Commandments displays to be put on classroom walls. A display of the Ten Commandments would not be unconstitutional if it were displayed with other documents of historical significance, like the Constitution, the Magna Carta, and the Declaration of Independence.

Rather than find a way to properly display the plaques, the Muldrow Public School administration crumbled. The FFRF had bullied the Muldrow school officials and won. Then they had the audacity to call those opposed to their demands a "religious mob."

On August 6, 2013 another school, this time in the small town of Cullman, Alabama, stood against the demands of the FFRF, when in a letter to the superintendent the FFRF demanded that an upcoming prayer caravan be canceled. This was the third annual caravan that included stopping at each of the district's 29 schools and praying for the students, teachers, and staff. Superintendent Coleman had helped to organize the event and had posted it on the school's web site.

Instead of caving into FFRF's demands, Coleman hosted a press conference where he stated, "I know 'fear' can be a very strong deterrent to doing what is right... We have and will continue to respond respectfully, but it would be a mistake to take our 'kindred spirit' for fear. We are not afraid, and we are not alone. We have the support of millions in America who are ready to take a stand with those of us in Cullman County."[72]

Once Superintendent Coleman refused to back down, Governor Robert Bentley of Alabama expressed public support for the prayer event and for Superintendent Billy Coleman's participation, which had been criticized. The prayer caravan took place as scheduled on Saturday August 10, 2013, and more than 1,000 people showed up for the event. In the two previous years, the event had been modestly attended.

What Happened in the Realm of the Spirit?

Our country was founded by strong believers who felt it their duty to teach their children from the Bible and an integral part of that biblical teaching was the Ten Commandments. Enter the secular humanists, also known as the Progressives, who wanted to "free" our children from the confines of the religious teaching of Christianity. After all, religion was too restrictive for a child and hampered his or her creative thinking. Progressives knew that as long as Christians had an internal moral code they would never fall prey to socialism and eventually communism. Any reminder of moral absolutes, whether taught by a Christian teacher or displayed as a plaque in a classroom, would be a determent to the development of a child ready to embrace a collective form of government.

The Supreme Court decision to remove the display of the Ten Commandments from the eyes of our children dealt a double blow to the morals of our youth in two distinct ways. First was the removal of the First Commandment: "You shall have no other gods before me" (Exodus 20:3). That was paramount. Progressives wanted a child who put every religion on equal footing and could not tolerate any thought that there could be only one God. Secondly, the Ten Commandments are written reminders of the God-given moral restraints we are to observe as individuals and are required if we live in a free society. The ultimate goal for a secular humanist was to have children who will rely on the government for their moral direction and for their livelihood.

God help us to stand up for what is right in this country and not back down. Let us pray for more people who will take a stand for righteousness.

Prayer of Repentance for Allowing the Ten Commandments to Be Removed from Public Schools

Father, I come to You in the Name of Jesus. First of all, I repent for the Ten Commandments being removed from the classrooms of America.

Now I remind You of the covenant You made with Your people when You said You would write Your laws in their hearts and You would write them on their minds, and their sins and lawless acts You would remember no more. (Jeremiah 31:34; Hebrews 10:17.) With thankfulness, I remind You of that covenant and believe You for the fulfillment of Your Word. Write Your laws on their hearts and in the minds of our children. Turn our educational system to be the instrument that helps to write Your laws in their hearts and minds.

When the apostle Paul prophesied "all of Israel will be saved," I believe that he was also speaking of the children of the nation of America. I believe that all of America will be saved. There will come a deliverer who will turn godlessness away from us and You will keep your covenant with us and will take away our sins. (Romans 11:26–27.)

You said that where the Spirit of the Lord is there is freedom. I pray for the Spirit of the Lord to invade our educational system so that true freedom may be experienced by all. (2 Corinthians 3:16–17). I pray in Jesus Name. Amen.

Prophetic Declarations

1. I declare that as a believer in Jesus I walk in the commandment He gave to love toward others, especially those who may be considered my enemy and the enemy of my children. All my prayers for the educational system in this country and all my actions will be governed by love. (2 John 5.)

2. I declare that there will be no other God beside the one true God, the Creator of heaven and earth. There will be no other gods above You. T8he children in America will serve only You. (Exodus 20: 3.)

3. The children in this nation walk with You and keep Your commandments. Your commandments will be bound around their necks. When they walk, those commandments will guide them, when they sleep, those commandments will watch over them, when they awake, the commandments will speak to them. For Your commandments are a lamp and a light. (Proverbs 6:20–23.)

4. I proclaim that all children in our schools will have no other gods before them. (Exodus 20:3.)

5. I proclaim that the children in this nation and in particular those in our schools will not serve idols nor will they bow down to worship false gods; whether that idol be man, secular humanism, false religion or any artifact fashioned by man's hand for the purpose of worship. (Exodus 20:4.) I bind all idolatrous worship in any form in our schools.

6. I proclaim that the Name of God will be reverenced above all other names. The Name of Jesus will be lifted up in the schools and lives of the students in this land. (Exodus 20:7; John 12:32.)

7. I proclaim that the schools in this nation will honor the Sabbath day and keep it holy. (Exodus 20:8)

8. I proclaim that the children in our schools will be taught to honor their fathers and their mothers. They will be taught to love and honor the forefathers of our nation who have fought to preserve this country and make it free. (Exodus 20:12; Luke 18:20.)

9. We love and keep Your commandments and Your love is given to us for a thousand generations.

10. I proclaim that there will be no murder in our schools in America. Destruction and death are far from us. (Exodus 20:13; Psalm 91:10.)

11. I proclaim that our schools will honor the institution of marriage between a man and a woman. Adultery, fornication, sexual perversion, pornography, and other forms of sexual deviation will be removed from our schools. Our children will be taught sexual purity. (Exodus 20:14; Leviticus 20:13.)

12. I declare that all forms of sexual perversion and profit from sexual trade of any sort are bound and cannot operate in our schools. (2 Corinthians 6:17.)

13. I proclaim that all forms of stealing, cheating, and dishonest gain will be far from our schools and our children. Our children will be taught to give an honest day's work for an honest wage. (Luke 3:14.)

14. I proclaim that our children in America's schools are taught not to covet but to work for what they achieve. (Exodus 20:17.)

PHYSICAL PLACE OF REPENTANCE

Location for National Repentance:

The Supreme Court of the United States, Washington, DC.

Location for Local Repentance:

The State Supreme Court of your respective states is the first place to pray. Many of the court cases that have affected our public school systems were first taken to the state supreme courts and were given a favorable ruling prior to being turned over to the next level of court or to the Supreme Court.

If you are located in or near one of the ten District Courts or a Court of Appeals, it would be good to travel to that location for repentance. A good place to look for the courthouse buildings in and near your state is:

www.USCourts.gov/court_locator/courtwebsites.aspx

35 Entry Point # 7: Evolution in Public Schools

In June 18, 2013, Louisiana Governor Bobby Jindal signed a bill into law that allowed students to gather for prayer before and after school and during 'non-instructional times.' The law also stated that school employees, parents and community members may attend such prayer times.

Governor Jindal had once again crossed the line by offending Louisianans who strive for a secular educational system. This was not Jindal's first time to get in trouble with the secularists. On June 11, 2008, he signed what is known as the Louisiana Science Education Act (LSEA) into effect. Three times the Louisiana State Legislature has tried to overturn it; each effort has met with defeat. LSEA allows a local school board to determine if creationism can be taught to the students in their respective school districts. The law does not mandate the teaching of creationism but rather gives permission for a teacher to use supplemental materials to present creationism as a belief that some people endorse.

The scientific community is in an uproar over the prospect of creationism being presented in classrooms and has resulted in those who believe in evolution doing a lot of arm waving and name-calling. It might be well for us to remember that those who believe in evolution consider themselves intelligent and are supposedly the brightest minds in our nation. Yet, the tactics of the scientific community has not changed for the past 150 years. They attack and spread what I call *Ignorant Dust*—accusing everyone who does not believe in evolution of being ignorant, backward, uninformed, stupid, and a laughingstock to those who are educated.

In 2013, the Botanical Society of America conference was held in New Orleans in a direct attempt to affront the people of Louisiana and Governor Jindal on his own doorstep. As a public forum for evolutionists, many of the leading scientists of our day attended the conference and took the opportunity to decry LSEA and Governor Jindal. In a public appeal to the governor, Zack Kopplin, a nineteen-year-old Rice University student who has led a campaign against LSEA, made statements that demeaned Governor Jindal and anyone else who believed in the theory of evolution.

Kopplin stated that creationism was not science because, "Science is the way we explain natural phenomena. Scientific explanations can be tested, and these tests can be repeated time and time again and will produce the same results. Creationism is an un-testable metaphysical story. Evolution, on the other hand, is a valid scientific theory that meets all the requirements of science."[73]

While Kopplin continues his speech with similar statements, it is interesting to note that he is stating that evolution is a scientific fact that meets scientific requirements, which it does not. Evolution is a theory, no more and no less. Kopplin also states that scientific explanations can be tested time and time again with the same results, which again is not true. In today's world of science, the coming of age of quantum physics allows different results for tests, according to the observer. Not that scientists are going to agree with creationists any time in the near future; however, it will be interesting to see how they explain the new discoveries that are being made every day in the scientific community. Scientific discoveries could be very different in the near future.

Our prayer is with the Louisiana Legislature and with those who will stand against the tide of name-calling and resist "Ignorant Dust" fallout when someone makes a stand for creationism to be presented in our public schools.

The Removal of Creationism from Schools

The groundwork for only the theory of evolution to be taught in our public schools was put in place in the 1880s when Darwin's book, *Origin of Species*, found favor as a theory among American progressive educators. The idea of man evolving from an animal was something that secularists could embrace because it appealed to the mind of reason and also because they didn't believe in God in the first place, so how could He be a creator? From that point on, it was just a matter of time until the content of what could be taught in regard to man's origin would be tested in the American court system.

Two major court decisions resulted in the teaching of creationism to be removed from our classrooms and replaced with the teaching of the theory of evolution. The first event took place in 1925 at the Scopes trial; the second happened in 1987, when the courts ruled in *Edwards vs. Aguillard* that the theory of evolution alone could be taught in all American public schools.

The Scopes trial, which came to be known as the Scopes Monkey Trial, was a fabricated, deliberately staged media production intended to test in the courts the validity of teaching evolution. The Progressives knew that most of the people in our nation believed in creationism and had to be persuaded by some act to think otherwise.

Science teacher John Thomas Scopes, who believed in and taught evolution, agreed to be arrested for teaching evolution in his classroom. Which was in direct violation of a Tennessee law called the Butler Act, which stated it was unlawful to teach anything but creationism. The Scopes trial took place in Dayton, Tennessee.

The court ruled in favor of creationism and John Thomas Scopes, found guilty, was fined $100—which was a mere slap on the wrist. His conviction was later overturned on a technical error. Two famous lawyers, Williams Jennings Bryan and Clarence Darrow, stood face-to-face in the courtroom and the drama unfolded.

Bryan, a Christian who considered himself an expert on the Bible, allowed himself to take the witness stand. Darrow, who strongly supported the theory of evolution, humiliated and outsmarted Bryan in the cross-examination. While the Scopes trial did not overtly prove to be a defeat for Christians, it did mar the Christian image and pave the way for the 1987 court decision that evolutionism would be taught in public schools to the exclusion of even mentioning creationism.

In 1987, the United States Supreme Court ruled in *Edwards vs. Aguillard* that a Louisiana law requiring creation science to be taught in public school classrooms was unconstitutional and was intended to promote a particular religion. In support of Aguillard, 72 scientists who had been awarded the Nobel Peace Prize for their accomplishments, plus 17 state academies of science and seven other scientific organizations filed briefs with the court in support of the teaching of evolution, opposing creationism because they believed it promoted the doctrines of the Church.

What Happened in the Realm of the Spirit?

Throughout history, the idea of man evolving from lower life forms has appealed to the intellect. Somehow man can reason with his mind, to the exclusion of his spirit, that man could evolve, regardless of the lack of scientific evidence to fully support his conviction.

The significance of this entry point is that if man was not created by God, he no longer had to answer to a creator for the deeds done in this life. When a person is taught that he is free from responsibility, he can do anything and not have to pay the consequences.

In Romans 1:28–32, the apostle Paul says:

**"Furthermore, since they did not think it worthwhile to retain the knowledge of God, he gave them over to a depraved mind, to do what ought not to be done. They have become filled with every kind of wickedness, evil, greed and depravity. They are full of envy, murder, strife, deceit and malice. They are gossips, slanderers, God-haters, insolent, arrogant and boastful; they invent ways of doing evil; they disobey their parents; they are senseless, faithless, heartless, and ruthless. Although they know God's righteous decree that those who do such things deserve death, they not only continue to do those very things, but also approve of those who practice them."
Romans 1:28-32.**

It sounds like Paul spent time in an American high school classroom!

Charles Darwin's book, ***Origin of Species***, was published in England in 1859, but it took another thirty years for Darwin's theory of evolution to move on to the American educational scene as an idea that would improve education. When it arrived, there was a receptive vehicle with the educational humanists, who continually looked for innovative ways to introduce evolution into the minds of our children.

The educational organization that swallowed the theory of evolution hook, line, and sinker and brought it to the public schools was a special committee that had been formed in the 1880s as a subset of the NEA called the National Council of Education. As an elite educational think tank of educational power brokers, the committee met to discuss innovative trends in progressive (liberal) education. One of the most well-known members of the committee was John Dewey.

They liked the idea of evolution but didn't know how to best introduce the concept to teachers who would then teach the idea to children of Christian parents who would certainly object. To liberate the mind of the child was foremost in the minds of the progressive gatekeepers. Any child held under bondage by religion or more specifically, the Christian religion, needed freedom. However difficult the task, the liberal thinkers felt that to promote evolution in the public school classrooms would be the quickest way to remove the students from a belief in God.

These men truly believed evolution would have positive effects on education as the students were liberated. They saw religious influence as detrimental to a child's ability to learn. Children should be allowed freedom to learn apart from God, who expected obedience. The mind, in order to learn properly, had to be liberated from the concept of God, mainly the Christian concept of God.

Slowly prodding along over the next thirty years, the first opportunity came in the form of a court trial; just like so many of the entry points, the very courts that were set in place to protect and preserve our freedoms, were used against us to promote a secular society apart from God. So the idea to teach evolution to the exclusion of creationism was born and carried through to its completion.

God continually speaks of His infinite greatness through His creation. Paul says, "For since the creation of the world God's invisible qualities—his eternal power and divine nature—have been clearly seen, being understood from what has been made, so that men are without excuse" (Romans 1:20). When the Creator in no longer acknowledged, He is no longer known. The result is that men become depraved.

Paul expresses the result in verses 24 and 25: "Therefore God gave them over in the sinful desires of their hearts to sexual impurity for the degrading of their bodies with one another. They exchanged the truth of God for a lie..." Could it possibly be that the dismissal of

God as the Creator of man resulted in an upheaval of sexual impurity? We have certainly witnessed that in our country.

One of the Christian philosophers of the Age of Enlightenment, Immanuel Kant, wrote: "Two things fill me with constantly increasing admiration and awe; the longer and more the earnestly I reflect on them: the starry heavens without and the moral law within." Kant recognized exactly what Paul described to us—the relationship a person has to the wonder of God's creation is in direct proportion to his internal moral law.

Francis Collins, the leading scientists in the Human Genome Project, is a believer. Dr. Collins said, "I believe God gave us two books. One is the book of God's Word—that's the Bible—and the other is the book of God's works, which is nature."[74]

The two go hand in hand. When our schools could no longer teach Creationism, our children lost their internal moral law. Man no longer held any moral responsibility to do what was right.

Prayer of Repentance for Allowing Only Evolution to Be Taught

Father, I come to You in the Name of Jesus. First of all, I ask Your forgiveness because the American educational system has not acknowledged You as the Creator of heaven and earth and all that lies therein.

I pray that revelation knowledge come to our educators and to our politicians so they acknowledge You in every classroom in America. May our children praise You because they see Your design in their lives and they know that they are fearfully and wonderfully made. (Psalm 139:14.)

God, show Yourself strong on behalf of those like the Louisiana Legislature and Governor Jindal who have taken a stand to allow creationism to be presented in public schools. Raise up other legislatures, governors, and educators who will take a stand to teach that You created man and woman and the heavens and the earth.

Let our children know that when the earth was formless and empty, darkness was over the surface of the deep and the Spirit of the living God hovered over the waters. Then God spoke and there was light, there was day, the waters were separated from the land, vegetation came forth, the stars were commanded in place and the living creatures were made. Then You capped Your creation when You made man and woman. (Genesis 1,2.) You brought forth man and woman to serve You and to commune with You. You poured out Your Spirit out on all flesh so that we would know the one true and living God, the Creator of heaven and earth. I pray this in the mighty Name of Jesus. Amen.

Prophetic Declarations

1. I declare that the students in America's classrooms will remember their Creator in the days of their youth. (Ecclesiastes 12:1.)

2. I declare that the educators in America will humble themselves before the Almighty God in their classrooms and in their lives, and that God will give grace to them and redeem our land. (1 Peter 5:5.)

3. I declare that our students will know that "In the beginning God created the heavens and the earth." (Genesis 1:1.)

4. I declare and decree that our teachers and students will know Jesus as the image of the invisible God, the firstborn over all creation. For by him all things were created; things in heaven and on earth, visible and invisible, whether thrones or powers or rulers or authorities; all things were created by him and for him. He is before all things, and in him all things hold together. And he is the head of the body, the church; he is the beginning and the firstborn from among the dead, so that in

everything he might have the supremacy. (Colossians 1:15–18.)

5. I declare and decree that God has set eternity in the hearts of men; and they will fathom what God has done from beginning to end. (Ecclesiastes 3:11.)

6. I declare and decree that all children in this nation, in view of God's mercy, will offer their bodies as living sacrifices, holy and pleasing to God—which is their spiritual act of worship. Our children will not be conformed any longer to the pattern of this world, but be transformed by the renewing of their minds. Then they will be able to test and approve what God's will is—his good, pleasing and perfect will. (Romans 12:1–2.)

7. I declare and decree that that the wrath of God will be revealed from heaven against all godlessness and wickedness of men who suppress the truth, which God has made plain to them. For since the creation of the world God's invisible qualities—his eternal power and divine nature—have been clearly seen, being understood from what has been made, so that men are without excuse.(Romans 1:18–20.)

8. I declare and decree that the Name of the Lord will be praised. He will be praised from the heavens and in the heights above…Kings of the earth and all nations, your princes and rulers, young men and maidens, old men and children will praise the Lord. Let them praise the Name of the Lord, for his Name alone is exalted; his splendor is above the earth and the heavens. He has raised up for his people a horn, the praise of all his saints, of Israel, the people close to his heart. Praise the Lord. (Psalm 148:1,11–14.)

9. I declare and decree that the Good News will be preached to all creation. (Mark 16:15.)

10. I declare and decree that as Paul and Barnabas warned the people of Lystra not to worship them because they had healed the man with the crippled feet, neither shall our children

worship the gods of this world. I say that our children will receive the Good News of the Gospel and they will turn from worthless things to the living God, who made heaven and earth and sea and everything in them. (Acts 14:8,14–15.)

Physical Place of Repentance

Location for National Repentance:

Where the Scopes trials were conducted at the country court house in Dayton, Tennessee.

The Supreme Court of the United States, Washington, DC.

The ACLU is the organization that brought the case to court their main office is at 4301 Connecticut Ave. NW, Suite 434, Washington, DC.

Location for Local Repentance

Choose any county or local courthouse and pray at that location.

36 Entry Point # 8: The National Education Association (NEA)

One of the best metaphors to describe the NEA is that of a huge river with the source in Washington, DC. It winds through every state in our union right through the main street of every town. Its tributaries branch out into every school. This river, which started out with great intentions, quickly became polluted as men and women with academic brilliance and no spiritual depth saw it as a means of reaching into every school and providing the water of socialism and anti-god teachings to every child in America. The NEA continues to meander through every school in this great nation promoting its agenda of abortion, secularism, evolution, socialism, and climate change.

How could a great professional organization become such a monster? Samuel Blumenfeld, an educator and a strong advocate of phonics-based reading programs, labels the NEA as the Trojan Horse in American Education. He wrote:

"The NEA is probably the most intellectually dishonest organization in America. It is part union, part professional organization, and part political party. Its object is to control Congress, the fifty state legislatures, the Democratic Party, the curriculum in all the schools, public and private, and the entire teaching profession. Its interest in academics is subordinate to its radical political and social ends."[75]

Whew! That's a mouthful! Because the NEA is so huge and wields such a major influence in our society, a special force of intercessors is needed to pray with all diligence.

With the exception of the first few years of the NEA's existence, the ideas they advanced have been gleaned from educators who promoted secular humanism entangled with socialists and communist views and who regarded man as the measure of himself and in no need of God. Many of its members are not socialists but because of the magnitude of the organization, are powerless to stand against NEA policies. To underestimate this organization's influence over our children would be to our peril. Strategic prayer is an absolute necessity.

With over 2.7 million members, the NEA is the largest labor union in the United States consisting of teachers, administrators, school support staff, and anyone else who is associated with our educational system and wants to join. This includes textbook suppliers and other vendors who have a profit motive for belonging. The main NEA building that houses the national offices in Washington, DC is strategically located on prime real estate at 16th St. NW. Officials brag that the building is one of less than 100 "green" buildings in the city. Along with the main building, each state has a NEA building located somewhere near the campus of their state capitol building where local NEA employees are housed.

In the same proximity of the NEA building in DC, are the offices of the *National Geographic* magazine and Planned Parenthood, two major promoters of evolution and abortion in our country. Years ago, I drove past the Planned Parenthood office and saw three people kneeling in silent protest. How grateful I was that there are those who will take time out of their schedules to combat the idol of Molech and his forces of darkness. Just being in the proximity of the major idolatrous institutions brings a sense of the spiritual darkness concentrated in one location. It also gives one a better perspective on the extent of the battle needed to be addressed in order to change our nation's educational system.

The sad thing is that the NEA's influence didn't start out as a negative one. From 1857 to about 1900, the NEA was a gathering place where a handful of well-meaning educators and administrators met professionally to share ideas that would enhance their teaching methods. Presentations at meetings dealt with improved methods of instruction and honing teaching skills. What worked for one teacher might well work for another and material one teacher developed could be shared with other teachers.

The goal was to produce better teachers by sharing insights and connecting with leaders in the educational field. Teachers wanted to be professional and wanted their students to achieve a high academic level of learning, so they networked. It was a humble beginning with the best of intentions. Its metamorphous occurred 1893 to 1918 as the NEA began to propose educational policy for our nation's schools.

In 1918, the NEA leaders felt that by locating their headquarters to Washington, DC, they could better influence educational policy. The NEA remained a professional organization until 1972. At which time, because of their intense lobbying activities, forced membership, and a new NEA constitution, they came under the scrutiny of the IRS and consequently were reclassified as a labor organization.

As public schools were created to form a new social order, the NEA was created to help facilitate that dream. In 1934, Dr. Willard Givens, a California school superintendent, addressed the 72nd NEA annual convention. "We are convinced that we stand today at the verge of a great culture," he said. "But to achieve these things many drastic changes must be made. A dying laissez-faire must be completely destroyed, and all of us, including the owners, must be subjected to a large degree of social control."[76]

After Dr. Givens called for the destruction of free enterprise, he was named executive secretary of the NEA—a post he held for 17 years. The NEA pours millions of dollars into election campaigns to elect those candidates who will support not only their union but also the liberal socialistic causes they hold near and dear. Here are a few of the controversial issues the NEA not only endorses but also provides teaching curriculum so that teachers can influence the students in their classrooms:

- Sex education

- Abortion, defined as a woman's right to choice

- Earth Day, reverence to Mother Earth

- Climate change

- Early childhood education, the current push is to lower the age of mandatory school attendance to four

- Gun control

- Reproductive rights

- Evolution

- Humanism (the Humanist Manifesto was written by John Dewey and other members of the NEA).

From the beginning, leadership of the NEA was held by those who were deemed as humanists, who saw man's mind as the highest manifestation of the universal divine spirit. They supported the belief that man's law is God's law and man's government is supreme, for there can be no other law above it. Basically, man is god and man's mind is a microcosm of God's mind. No provision was to be made for educating the spirit of a child, the mind was supreme. Although leadership changed within the NEA, the socialists and humanistic agenda has never changed.

The NEA leaders seized on the theory of evolution as a way to create an even wider chasm between religion and education. Man could be linked downward to animals and not upward to a living God. Evolution allowed the promotion of teaching by conditioning rather than by understanding.

The 1920s and 1930s were a perilous age for America as the fight for the soul of our nation played out on in the hearts of many Americans. We experienced a terrific economic depression. Many people were out of work. They eked out a living off family farms, accepted government assistance, or the help from those who served meals at soup kitchens. During this time some of the brightest minds entertained the belief that America would be better under a socialist or a communist form of government.

Also during this time, reformers like John Dewey realized that if they were to create a socialist America, they would have to start with reforms in the classrooms. Although Dewey's ideas were not new— the Enlightenment Age had fostered them for over one hundred years earlier—he was one of the first in America to seize education as a vehicle to revolutionize this country. We saw earlier how he started first by presenting the ideas to leading academics, who then presented them to professors in Ivy League universities. They in turn presented them to professors in state colleges, who presented them to students training to become teachers in schools in rural and urban areas of America. Those teachers then presented the ideas to the children sitting at their school desks. It was the trickle-down effect and given enough time, it worked.

As new leaders like John Dewey emerged, they were able to change the NEA ideology and the NEA agenda began the promotion of the education of a child for the good of society. Today the NEA's agenda is almost totally socialistic and political.

No other organization wields as much power over schools in the US. The whole public educational system is held in the grip of the NEA and until this organization is dealt with on a spiritual level we will not be able to see transformation in public schools. Christians have for the most part abandoned the organization on the governing level.

What Happened in the Realm of the Spirit?

From the first meetings of the precursor to the National Education Association, the teachers and administrators began to inquire about the establishment of a national organization that would help them out in making decisions and unify all the school systems in the nation. While it sounded like a wonderful idea, it was ultimately not in the best interest of our nation and especially not in the best interest of the children of this nation.

We found ourselves in the same situation as when elders of Israel came to Samuel and asked him to appoint a king to rule over them. Samuel prayed and the word the Lord gave Samuel was, **"Listen to all that the people are saying to you; it is not you they have rejected, but they have rejected me as their king....Now listen to them; but warn them solemnly and let them know what the king who will reign over them will do."**

(1 Samuel 8:6–22.)

Later Samuel elaborated on the consequences of Israel's having a king. Samuel told them that a king would take their sons and daughters and make them work for him. Eventually a king would require more and more of them and their children. Their children would have to fight for the king and the people would become slaves of the king.

Prayer of Repentance for Allowing the NEA to Be a Powerful Anti-God Influence over Our Children.

Father, in the Name of Jesus I come to You. First of all, I repent for allowing the NEA to be established as an institution that would feed the children of our nation anti-God and anti-American propaganda. Father, I ask for Your mercy over our schools. Raise up Godly leaders and organizations that will reinstate the foundational Christian values that made America great. I call out leaders who will lead our schools, children, and teachers in the way of Godliness, embracing patriotism and the truth of Your Word.

Shine Your light in every nook and cranny of our schools and rout out every vestige of evil. Deliver us from those who would harm the minds and spirits of our youth. Restore us to Your direction for this nation's educational system and give us Godly leaders who will hear Your voice and obey You.

I remind You that when Josiah stood before You and repented when the Book of the Law was found and he realized that his people had followed idols, You spared the land. (2 Kings 22.) I stand before You in repentance for allowing all the idols and false gods to be set up in our schools through the NEA and I ask You to spare America. Josiah desecrated the high places where the priests had sacrificed to idols. He tore down the altar to Molech so that the people could not sacrifice their children in the fire. (2 Kings 23:8.) I will tear down those false gods and renew my covenant with You. I pray this in Jesus Name. Amen.

Prophetic Declarations

1. I declare that parents will rise up and teach their children Your wisdom and Your understanding. Then the nations of the earth will hear about our success and will say, "Surely this great nation is a wise and understanding people." Our children

will follow Your commandments so that they will take possession of this land. There has never been a nation so great as ours with wisdom and understanding. Our God is near us when we pray. No other nation is so great as to have righteous decrees and laws. I will watch myself closely so that I will not forget the things my eyes have seen or let them slip from my heart as long as I live. I will teach them to my children and to their children after them. Our children will revere You as long as they live in the land. (Deuteronomy 4:5–10.)

2. I declare that the days of unrighteous rule over our schools and our children is over. The National Education Association is not the ruler over us, our children, or our schools. I bring the authority of the education of our children back to the parents and I declare and decree that the parents will take responsibility for their children. (Deuteronomy 4:9.)

3. I declare that You will drive away those who seek to destroy Your sheep and lead them astray. Then You will gather the remnant of Your flock and will bring them back to You. You will place shepherds over them who will tend them. (Jeremiah 23:1–4.)

4. I declare that as the prophets recognized the poison in the pot of stew, our children will recognize the poison being fed them and will spew it out. As you gave Elisha the remedy for the poison, You reveal to Your prophets today the remedy for the poison in our educational system. (2 Kings 4:39–41.)

5. I declare that You will vindicate us from those who would lead our children astray. (Luke 17:1–2.)

6. I declare that Jesus, is the gate and these little children will come to You and find safe pasture. (John 10:9.)

7. I declare that though the thief has come to steal, kill, and destroy our children, You, Jesus, have come that they might have life and have it to the full. (John 10:10.)

8. I declare that God will raise up organizations in our schools who will be good shepherds over our teachers and children and will lead them in the way of Godliness. (John 10:11.)

9. I declare, Woe to those who call evil good and good evil, who put darkness for light and light for darkness, who put bitter for sweet and sweet for bitter. Woe to those who are wise in their own eyes and clever in their own sight. As a tongue of fire licks up straw and as dry grass sinks down in the flames, so their roots will decay and their flowers blow away like dust. (Isaiah 5:20–24.)

10. I declare that when our children drink deadly poison, it will not harm them. (Mark 16:18.)

PHYSICAL PLACE OF REPENTANCE

Location for National Repentance:

Main office building of the NEA is at 1201 16th St. NW, Washington, DC.

Location for State Repentance:

Each state has an NEA office building, usually located near that state's capitol building. Find your state NEA building and pray at that site.

37 Entry Point # 9: Rewriting History

Madalyn Murray O'Hair filed one of the first lawsuits against prayer and Bible reading in all public schools in America. She initially wanted her lawsuit also to prohibit certain textbooks. As an atheist, one she found particularly insulting was her son's history book, *The Story of Nations*, which contained references to Christianity. "All the religion in the book was given as fact," she argued. One of her major objections was a picture of the Last Supper.[77]

Later she decided that textbook censorship was of secondary concern and settled on her primary focus of eliminating prayer and Bible reading. Although O'Hair refocused, the textbook industry took notice of the court cases and began its evolution toward a secular approach to the curriculum they produced. The newly trained teachers and curriculum writers had sat under humanists teachers and were ready to rewrite history.

Today, no subject is exempt from the anti-God message of secularism that has penetrated the very core of school curricula. What isn't overtly stated in our textbooks is omitted. Once man is set up as a god, he then has no accountability to be a moral person, other than to himself. Man becomes the end unto himself. This is the dangerous lie that is being perpetrated on our school children day after day.

As an algebra teacher, I remember the distain I felt regarding all the references I saw in math texts to witches, warlocks, devils, and goblins in written problems. In an effort to steer away from Christianity, the authors felt totally safe in composing problems dealing with the occult. Those references were clearly desensitizing the students to God and introducing them to the occult. Scary as it is, the occult references had no problem passing the religious separation clause of the Constitution that references to Christianity continually fail.

Socialism is another "ism" prevalent in today's textbooks that undermines the free enterprise system that has made America great. Textbooks often shy away from the mere use of the term *free market*. At the core of socialism is the belief that businesses should not be run for profit. Businesses should exist for the good of the people and in almost all cases, should be owned and administered by the government. America has prospered because a man or woman could work hard and earn not only a decent living but could also make a profit.

Currently one of the most blatantly anti-Christian history textbook series available to junior high school and high school students is *A People's History of the United States*, written by socialist Howard Zinn. To make the series more classroom friendly, Zinn includes a video version of the book. American history is explained in the framework of class and race conflict. To make sure that the content is used in many classrooms, the content is made more accessible and teacher friendly through free downloadable modules for teachers to use in their classrooms. Zinn's series is not the only example. The textbook industry is replete with socialist and humanistic materials.

The current trend is to create curricula for students as early as kindergarten that incorporate education on sexual diversity and sexual preference. Often, unless parents raise objections or seek collective legal action, the curriculum is adopted without hesitation. That's why it is important to be informed of what is being promoted as curriculum at the federal, state, district, and local levels.

How Is History Altered?

One of the most common ways of altering history is simply to omit pertinent historical facts. Most offensive and likely to be edited out are references to Christianity, in particular as it relates to US history. If a child is never told that our Founding Fathers were godly men and women who came to this country in order to worship God according to the dictates of their own conscience, they are then more open to the suggestion that our country was founded by men and women who came to this country out of greed.

It might be interesting to note that in some history textbooks there is but a bare mention of President George Washington. Nothing is said of his outstanding character and his devotion to God, while great mention is made of such personalities as Marilyn Monroe. What is the purpose of background information being omitted on our first and most influential president? By omission, the student assumes that the information is not important. As believers, we know George Washington's devotion to God is of vital importance in preserving the religious heritage of this nation and needs to be included in every historical textbook.

In some cases, whole class subjects are omitted. A recent survey by the National Assessment of Educational Progress (NAEP) found that in 2010 only 67 percent of students reported studying the Constitution at all. Many reported that there was insufficient civics in the curriculum, to prepare them to pass the test for US citizenship. If a person does not know how our government works, how officials are elected, how the three branches of government—legislative, executive, and judicial—balance each other in power and how our government came into being, then how can he be expected to maintain one of the greatest governments in the world? Our government will crumble if our citizens are not taught to value what we have and how to maintain it. Civics needs to be a vital part of every curriculum.

Recently I saw a tee shirt for sale that said, "I graduated from a liberal college and turned out a conservative." It's truly a miracle for a student to go through four years of liberal teaching and hold on to conservative views. The most likely scenario is that the student, educated as a liberal, entered the work force and then became conservative. US institutions of higher learning are bastions of liberal thought. My son has a master's degree in political science from a state university. Three times in his academic career he was required to read the **Communist Manifesto**. The Bible was never mentioned.

The one book my son felt everyone should be required to read, at gunpoint if necessary, was ***The Prize: The Epic Quest for Oil, Money and Power***. Although *The Prize* by Daniel Yergin won a Pulitzer Prize in 1992, it was a stellar work on free markets but never met approval for required reading. As Mary Beth Hicks so aptly stated in her book ***Don't Let the Kids Drink the Kool-Aid***.

> "The Leftists don't have to have children. They can steal ours. And to win they don't have to turn our children into angry revolutionaries. They just have to do exactly what they are doing—shape our kids into a generation completely ignorant of the principles that have made America the extraordinary nation it is, and fill them with so much worry over so-called crises (from global warming to the childhood obesity epidemic) that they'll naturally let the government step in and take care of us all."[78]

By rewriting history and presenting the new curriculum filled with humanistic, atheistic, and socialistic thought in incremental doses, children end up believing or being tolerant of beliefs and ideas that undermine our Judeo-Christian values. Parents have a huge task to teach their children how to counter the subtleties of tainted curriculum. Many parents are unaware of what is being taught.

Another means of altering history is through writing curriculum that interprets history through the lens of humanistic beliefs. By humanists' standards, our forefathers were narrow-minded, prejudiced, bigoted men and women who came to this country, not to seek religious freedom, but to seek riches. If a person doesn't know God, then how can we expect them to see God's hand in our history?

It's the difference between viewing with the mind as opposed to looking at history through the eyes of the Spirit, which Paul addresses when he said, **"The man without the Spirit does not accept the things that come from the Spirit of God, for they are foolishness to him, and he cannot understand them, because they are spiritually discerned" (1 Corinthians 2:14).** The battle between the human intellect and the Spirit still rages just as strongly today as it has since the beginning of time.

We are in a struggle for the minds of the children, teens, and young adults. Not just to teach them the correct facts of history, but to teach the Spirit behind the motives and actions of our forefathers. The rewriting of history is an entry point for the enemy. While not all curricula are wrought with historical errors and humanistic influence, much of it is.

What Happened in the Realm of the Spirit?

A 2009 Rasmussen Report poll measuring respondents' feelings about capitalism versus socialism, found that among adults under age thirty, 37 percent favor capitalism as a political and economic system, while 33 percent favor socialism. Roughly 30 percent are undecided.[79]

The Rasmussen Report should give all of us cause for alarm. The US is one of the few places on earth where a person can come to not only earn a living but make a profit by hard work and financial savvy. Our children are taught that Americans are consumers, big business exploits, ethical behavior depends on the circumstances, and homosexuality is a viable moral choice. It's all done through the curriculum of our school.

The process of indoctrination via curricula began in the early 1960s as the Supreme Court began accepting cases dealing with prayer and Bible reading in public schools. The classrooms became a battle grounds that required teachers to be more disciplinarians than instructors. The students, no longer responsible for their own behavior, were free to make moral decisions based on what was relevant to their situation.

We are currently in the third generation of students who have sat under liberal teaching and who are currently teachers, curriculum writers, classroom teachers, college professors, and administrators with liberal views. Within fifty plus years, we have witnessed firsthand the erosion of many of the fundamental principles that made America the leading nation in the world and a protector of freedom, to where we are now viewed as greedy aggressors.

The traditional family has broken down and socialism and humanism are now a way of life for most adults. With the foundation for rewriting history having been laid, and the introduction of humanism, atheism, and socialism into the curriculum, further erosion takes a much shorter time to register significant results.

Most students have twelve years of schooling plus whatever postsecondary education they may have taken, to turn them against Jesus and America. Because of what is being taught in the classroom, many graduates now believe that Christianity is no different than any other religion (this was one of John Dewey's objectives) and America is no different than any other country.

Humanism has entwined itself into the core of classroom instruction. We are in a battle for the minds and spirits of our children. Not just to teach them the correct facts of history, but to teach the spiritual motives and actions of our forefathers. The men and women who founded this country were those who allowed their values to dictate their actions. We have a rich heritage to pass to our children.

The Textbook Adoption Conundrum

Each state in the US must approve what textbooks are to be used in its classrooms. This review process is called *adoption.* Usually several textbooks are adopted in each subject and the local school boards then have the option to select from the state-adopted list. Textbooks rotate in the adoption process, one year history books will be adopted (this is usually when the most heated arguments occur), another year the adoption process might be for math books, and so on, until all the texts for the public school curriculums are rotated through the adoption process. Once a rotation is completed, the process starts all over again.

Every state school board is an entry point for curriculum, good or bad, to be allowed in the classrooms of its respective state. Throughout the years Texas and California have risen in importance in the textbook adoption process, because of the tremendous amount of textbooks they purchase each year. They also have the largest student enrollments. California has over 6.2 million students and Texas has over 5 million. Texas alone will spend almost $800 million on learning materials each year.[80]

The remaining 48 states will wait until Texas and California have selected the textbooks they will use and then often adopt the same ones, thereby avoiding the controversial fanfare that accompanies an adoption process. The result is that the content of most of our nation's textbooks is determined by the Board of Education of the two powerful states of Texas and California. Therefore, Texas and California are the primary entry points and are places that should be prayed over for this specific portal.

The battle between the liberals and the conservatives in Texas is featured in national media. When in the adoption of textbooks for courses like history and English literature come before the Texas School Board, the battles between the liberals and the conservatives often continue late into the night for days on end. The arguments are typically over such phrases as whether or not America should be called a democracy or a constitutional republic or whether the word *capitalism* should be replaced with the words *free enterprise system.*

Recently conservatives swayed the Texas board to allow questions on the evolution debate, when the board voted to approve a textbook that asked students to consider whether gaps in the fossil record and the complexity of the human cell can be explained by evolution. Why shouldn't our students be asked to give critical thought to the gaps in the teaching of evolution? The evolutionists do not want their agenda questioned. They want their theory to be taught as an absolute fact.

The Texas Board of Education became such a hotbed of controversy that in 2012 Texas voted to allow textbook decisions to be made at the local school district level, which took the centralized power away from the Texas Board of Education. Now each school district must make the decision for what textbooks to use in its classrooms. This decision made it more difficult to point to one location in Texas as a place for prayer and repentance, but it didn't lessen the need to consider Texas as one of the most important locations for both.

The Texas and California Departments of Education are two locations where prayer must be offered and where those who will pray must ask for forgiveness for allowing our textbooks to be stripped of references to our Judeo-Christian heritage and God. We should ask God to turn back the tide in our curricula include material that emphasize Godly character qualities, hold students accountable for their actions, teach respect for authority, a belief in God, and that are rich in Godly historical content.

Prayer of Repentance for Allowing History to Be Rewritten

Father, I come to you in the Name of Jesus. First of all, I ask You to forgive America for allowing the greatness of Your power, from being minimized in our classrooms and especially in the textbooks that are used to teach our children.

I realize that my battle is not against flesh and blood but against rulers, authorities and the powers of this dark world and against the spiritual forces of evil in the heavenly realms. Therefore, I pray that You rebuke the powers of deception and darkness that desires to invade the hearts and minds of our students.

I ask You to raise up textbook authors who will produce quality materials that will give a history of this country that will not only testify of great leaders that You empowered to lead America but will also testify to Your greatness in providing for us, protecting us and preserving this nation. I ask that You rearrange school boards, textbook adoption committees, and textbook companies to produce and adopt Godly textbooks for our schools. I pray that those whom You raise up will be salt and light to this nation.

Give Your people the gumption to speak out where we should and take a righteous stand for accurate historical recounts of the moral fortitude that made us great. Let us once more be a nation that honors and reverences the God who created us in His image. I thank You for hearing our prayers in the Name of Jesus. Amen.

Prophetic Declarations

1. I declare our children will be as Daniel who praised You for Your wisdom and power. You reveal deep and hidden things to our children and give knowledge and understanding in all kinds of literature and learning. (Daniel 2:20.)

2. I declare that Godly textbook writers will come to the

215

forefront as scholars who are well versed not only in historical facts but also are alive to the Spirit of the living God. Let their words be as the pen of a skillful writer. (Psalm 45:1.)

3. I declare that textbook adoption committees will be filled with Godly men and women of upstanding moral character who will represent You in America's history as the One who made us a great nation. (1 Timothy 2:1–2.)

4. I declare that textbook writers will come forth and rebuild the ancient walls that have been torn down. (Nehemiah 2:17–18.)

5. I declare that our children will know the truth and the truth will set them free. (John 8:32.)

6. I declare that this nation will have textbooks that will teach our children Your paths and will guide them in the truth, for You are God our Savior and our hope is in You all day long. (Psalm 25:4–5.)

7. I declare that the states will adopt only accurately-written, balanced material that will teach our children that the fear of the Lord is the beginning of wisdom. (Psalms 111:10.)

8. I declare that financiers will back only Godly well-written textbooks. (2 Corinthians 9:11.)

9. I declare that our textbooks will show throughout history that righteousness exalts a nation, but sin is a reproach to any people. (Proverbs 14:34.)

10. I declare that our children will be able to have easy access to online material that is well-written and Godly. (Mark 11:23–24.)

11. I declare that God will raise up film makers and documentarians who will produce Godly, well-written material that will appeal to our children and will teach them character and accurate historical facts. (Mark 11:23–24.)

12. I declare a new day of boldness for Christian teachers in our

classrooms. Their tongues will be like that of Balaam. They will only be able to bless our nation even though they may have been told to do otherwise. (Numbers 23:7–11.)

13. I declare that America has been called to be a free nation and we will not use that freedom to cause others to indulge in the sinful nature, but rather, serve one another in love. All material that teaches on sexual orientation will be removed from our classroom. (Galatians 5:13.)

14. All school curricula are historically accurate. (Deuteronomy 4:7-9.)

15. All school curricula are based on critical thinking skills. (Proverbs 8:30.)

16. The promotion of humanism, atheism, and socialism is exposed and is systematically removed from the curricula of America's schools. (Job 28:11.)

17. I call men of Godly integrity and upstanding moral character who will uphold Judeo-Christian values into the offices of state and local school boards. (1 Timothy 3:1–13.)

Physical Place of Repentance

Location for National Repentance:

The Texas State Board of Education in Austin, Texas:
Although this location is purely symbolic since Texas has opted to make the selection of their textbooks be determined on a local level, it is still important because of the vast number of textbooks Texas purchases.

Texas Education Agency
1701 N. Congress Ave.
Austin, TX 78701
tea.state.tx.us

The California State Board of Education in Sacramento, California:

The California State Board of Education still determines which textbooks will be adopted for the state of California. Therefore, the State Board of Education of California is one location for repentance.
Location:

California State Board of Education
1430 N. Street, Suite #5111
Sacramento, CA 95814
cde.ca.gov

Location for Local Repentance:

Every county has a school board. Find out where that local school board meets and pray at that location.

38 Entry Point # 10: National Department of Education

In 2001, I took (one of my first groups) fifteen intercessors to Washington, DC to pray for the United States. As a new group to the area, I felt that it was important for us to connect with established intercessors who were currently praying in DC. I called Sandy Grady, who had worked for years as a key intercessor for David Barton of WallBuilders.[81] I shared with Sandy my desire to pray at educational sites in DC. I will never forget that conversation.

"Nancy, everyone who comes to DC goes to the same places," she said. "They go to the White House, the Capitol building, the Washington Monument, and other famous landmarks. But I've never known a group to go to the National Department of Education. Please go there and pray. Our schools need our prayers and people don't think to include education in their prayer trips to DC. What you want to do will be hard, but don't back down."

Sandy's words never left me. Although I've taken a lot of groups to DC since that time to pray, I've never failed to take them to key sites connected with education so they can pray on sight with insight.

However, that first time was just as difficult as she'd predicted it would be. Over and over, I heard her words ring in my spirit, "Don't back down. Don't back down. Don't back down." I didn't.

Going to the National Department of Education and praying in front of the building is one thing, but to go inside and pray is another, which I soon discovered. In order to go inside the Department of Education building one must have an invitation from someone who works there. Somewhere I'd been given the name of a man from Oklahoma—Jim—who worked in the Department of Education, so I called him a couple of weeks before my group would be in DC and we had a nice chat. He agreed to host our group by giving us a tour of the building and then allowing us to have a brief moment in the building's small auditorium to pray. I hung up thinking everything was all set.

I called him several times the day of our visit. When he didn't return my calls, I was surprised. Time came for us to leave for the appointment and no response. Since I couldn't confirm my appoint with Jim, I had no assurance that we would even be allowed in the building once we got there. I gave those in my prayer group an option to stay behind if they were not up for any confrontation we might encounter. Eight people decided not to attend the *"iffy"* appointment. Now I had nine intercessors, including me. To be honest, I was the most scared of all. Sandy's words continued to play like a broken record in the back of my mind. "Don't back down. Don't back down."

We entered the National Department of Education building, went through security, and asked to speak to Jim. Instead of Jim, two burley security guards came to greet us. They demanded to know why we were there and what our relationship was with Jim. I told them we had come to pray for America's educational system and gave them the name of the man from Oklahoma. One man left and a few minutes later came back and told us that Jim was busy and couldn't meet with us.

I then asked if there was a room we could go to pray. The security men ushered us to a small auditorium where we placed chairs in a circle and began to pray for America's schools. I don't know if they realized after awhile that we were harmless, but about twenty minutes later, "Mr. Oklahoma" showed up and the security men disappeared. He confessed to me later that he had been afraid and had backed out (without telling me). He redeemed the time as he showed us around the building and introduced us to the head of the Department of Education as well as key people in the building. We ended up praying in every office, even the office of the head of the department. It was a victory that would not have happened without one seasoned intercessor telling me, "Don't back down. Don't back down."

I share that same admonition with you—no matter what circumstance you find yourself in as an intercessor for our schools and for our children, don't back down! It's not an easy task and certainly not for the faint of heart. But persistence and tenacity are paramount when taking on this giant.

Another thing I learned on that trip to the National Department of Education was this: always be up front with people and tell them that you came to pray. Later I learned to tell people that I came to pray in the Name of Jesus. It's amazing that for years, I had in my mind that this would invoke all kinds of negative responses, but it has done exactly the opposite. I've seen doors open wide when I say, "I came to pray in the Name of Jesus." It's liberating because I have been completely honest and as Corrie ten Boom once said, "You have proven that you have nothing behind your elbow."[82] An honest announcement allows me the freedom to exalt the One who called me to establish His kingdom on this earth.

The National Department of Education was signed into existence on October 17, 1979 by President Jimmy Carter, as a fulfillment of a campaign promise to the teacher labor unions. Many lawmakers and citizens felt that the formation of the Department of Education was in direct opposition to the Constitution of the United States. The Constitution granted all powers not specified in the Constitution to the states and since no mention is made of education in the Constitution, by default, that power was relegated to the states. With the formation of a federal department complete with a cabinet post, the education of our children came under the jurisdiction of the federal government.

The federal government is acutely aware that our schools are in a state of decline. They simply do not know what to do to redeem education as a whole. What the government does really well is to implement more programs that place restrictions and regulations on schools. Honestly, they are trying, but their efforts have met with dismal failure. President George W. Bush's educational program initiated through the National Department of Education called "No Child Left Behind" placed tremendous burdens on teachers, who had to implement individual instruction plans for every student in his and her classroom. It was too much and proved to be ineffective.

The Obama administration through the Department of Education, along with the Bill and Melinda Gates Foundation, has proposed Standard Core Curriculum (CCSSI), which sets academic standards at each grade level that a child must master in order to move to the next grade level. The initiative is funded by the Bill Gates Foundation in an effort to produce more high school graduates who are college and career ready (a popular phrase used by President Obama). Bill Gates originally funded specialized high schools, which proved to be ineffective in producing higher numbers of graduating students who were college and career ready. Gates then decided that the major contributing factor was teacher competency, which he couldn't address because of teacher unions.

The next best program was to implement standards that teachers would have to teach—hence, Common Core Curriculum. Common Core sets academic standards for each grade level. The Gates Foundation is pumping $354 million into the program, which sounds like a great thing—that a child has to meet certain requirements—but the truth is that the standards have been lowered to allow more children to pass to the next grade level.

Each state had the right whether or not it would choose to

implement Common Core Curriculum. So far Texas, Alaska, Nebraska, and Virginia have not approved it and Minnesota has not approved the math component. Of course there is money given to the states for implementation, which is a great incentive to accept Common Core or any other government-sponsored program. Just as Kansas in 1892 made the decision to turn over the education of their children to the state, the states that adopted Common Core Curriculum also made the decision to once again turn over the education of their children to the state.

No Child Left Behind and Common Core both put their emphasis on requiring more of schools, which in turn puts pressure on teachers. Teachers only have a small slice of time to influence a child. For the most part, teachers are already overworked and unable to incorporate more work into their busy school day. Neither program places any requirements on parents or local societies to make children college and career ready. Parents in many cases have left the responsibility of educating their children to the schools and to the government. Until the government addresses the root causes of the failed system, nothing will help. There will just be a lot of money spent with a modicum of results, if any.

What Happened in the Realm of the Spirit?

When all the elders of Israel gathered to together and came to Samuel they said, "You are old, and your sons do not walk in your ways; now appoint a king to lead us, such as all the other nations have." Their request displeased Samuel, but he agreed to take their petition to God in prayer. The Lord replied:

> **"Listen to all that the people are saying to you; it is not you they have rejected, but they have rejected me as their king. As they have done from the day I brought them up out of Egypt until this day, forsaking me and serving other**

gods, so they are doing to you. Now listen to them; but warn them solemnly and let them know what the king who will reign over them will do."

1 Samuel 8:7–9

Samuel told the people that the king who would reign over them would take their sons and daughters to make them serve the government. That is exactly what the National Department of Education does; it makes our schools serve the government and not the local people, who have the children in neighborhood schools. We educate our children to serve the government and not to become entrepreneurs, statesmen, leaders, capitalists, good mothers and fathers, or even good citizens. The federal government serves its own purpose and, because of the enormous weight of oversight, cannot efficiently affect local schools and neighborhoods. We have a king.

Prayer of Repentance for Allowing the NEA to Wield Power Over Our Educational System

Father, I come to You in the Name of Jesus. First of all, I repent of the sin of wanting a king or superior authority to rule over us and our children. You are our ruler and I acknowledge You as the One who gives authority to the family to educate our children in Your ways.

I ask You to cause parents to rise up and teach their children Your ways. Let them teach their children Your wisdom and understanding. Amen.

Prophetic Declarations

1. I declare that local communities will rise up and take responsibility for the education of the children in their schools. (Deuteronomy 4:9.)

2. I declare that the spirit of individualism that made this country great would be revived and our children will not be a slave to the government. (Genesis 9:5.)

3. I declare that the hearts of the fathers will be turned toward their children and the hearts of the children will be turned to their fathers, so You will restore our land and not strike it with a curse. (Malachi 4:6.)

4. I declare that the Mountain of the Lord will be established as chief among the mountains; it will be raised above the hills and peoples of the nation. (Micah 4:1.)

5. I declare that the National Department of Education will have a heart to serve the children and the people of America. (Proverbs 21:1.)

6. I declare that if the National Department of Education makes unjust laws or issues oppressive decrees to deprive the poor of their rights and withholds justice from the oppressed, there will be a day of reckoning and there will be no place to run for help. (Isaiah 10:1–3.)

7. I declare that this government is upon the shoulders of Jesus and He will be called Wonderful, Counselor, Mighty God. Everlasting Father, Prince of Peace. Of the increase of His government and peace there will be no end. He will reign on David's throne and over his Kingdom, establishing and upholding it with justice and righteousness from that time on and forever. The zeal of the Lord Almighty will accomplish this. (Isaiah 9:6–7.)

8. I declare that the kingdoms of the world have become the Kingdom of our Lord and of His Christ, and He will reign forever and ever. (Revelation 11:15.)

9. I declare that I will not have to fight this battle. I will take my position and stand firm and see the deliverance the Lord will give me this day. I will not be afraid or discouraged. I will go out to face the enemy and the Lord will be with me. (2 Chronicles 20:17.)

10. I declare that every school and every organization will see that I am called by the Name of the Lord and they will fear me. (Deuteronomy 28:10.)

PHYSICAL PLACE OF REPENTANCE

Location for National Repentance:

The National Education Department in Washington, DC has several offices. Listed here are the main buildings:

Lyndon Baines Johnson (LBJ)
Department of Education Building
400 Maryland Ave, SW
Washington, DC 20202

Potomac Center Plaza (PCP)
550 12th Street, SW
Washington, DC 20202

Capitol Place
555 New Jersey Ave, NW
Washington, DC 20208

1990 K Street, NW
Washington, DC 20006

Union Center Plaza (UCP)
830 1st Street, NE
Washington, DC 20202

L'Enfant Plaza
490 L'Enfant Plaza, SW, Room 2100A
Washington, DC 20202

Location for Local Repentance:
The state capitol in every state in America.

39 David and Goliath

braham Lincoln said, **"The philosophy of the schoolroom in one generation will be the philosophy of government in the next."** That has certainly been true in America as we see socialism and secularization of our educational system now as it is played out in our government and courts. To reform our schools by addressing the roots of our misdirection in prayer will also create a reformation of our nation.

Those of us who desire to restore God's place in our education system are the Davids and the school system is the Goliath. The statement David made to Goliath in the valley of Elah applies to us in a very real way.

"You come against me with sword and spear and javelin, but I come against you in the Name of the LORD Almighty, the God of the armies of Israel, whom you have defiled. This day the LORD will hand you over to me, and I'll strike you down and cut off your head. Today I will give the carcasses of the Philistine army to the birds of the air and the beasts of the earth, and the whole world will know

that there is a God in Israel. All those gathered here will know that it is not by sword or spear that the LORD saves; for the battle is the LORD'S and he will give all of you into our hands." 1 Samuel 17:45–47

The anti-God forces in our educational system are overconfident, over secure, and under effective, making the timing of a spiritual battle of utmost importance. Just as Goliath, they dare people to try to change the system. Yet, everyone from the office of the President of the United States to the classroom teacher knows that our education is a dismal failure when 25 percent of our public school graduates are illiterate. It is time to seize the opportunity. Intercessors can take back education from the domination of Baal and consequently the children of our nation from his influence.

Actually, our chances of felling Goliath, even in the natural, get better the larger Goliath grows. Best-selling author and military historian Max Boot in his classic book, ***Invisible Armies: An Epic History of Guerrilla Warfare from Ancient Times to the Present,*** gives small insurgent groups a more than fighting chance of bringing down huge military operations. The smaller groups cost less money than larger armies to maintain. They can travel to a location undetected and make a strike, and quickly retreat.

A larger army relies on its reputation, technology, past victories, and often outdated styles to engage the enemy. Over the last one hundred years American education has promoted man-made doctrines and taunted Christians by daring them to attack their policies. With our band of prayer warriors, we can win, if we fight with nonconventional weapons, keep our ranks tightly knit around a common purpose, and engage the enemy on a level in which they are not accustomed.

The American educational system is huge with a budget of $591 billion annually. Its strength lies in the size of the institution. It cannot move quickly and is the epitome of the works of the flesh just as Goliath was. Daily the system promotes propaganda that is anti-God, anti-American, anti-Christian, and anti-moral. But it has been ineffective. Too long they have taunted those who believe in God. It is time we took our place with full knowledge of who our God is and what He can do.

Os Hillman, a well-known author and speaker on faith at work, states in his book *Change Agent*, "It takes less than 3–5 percent of those operating at the tops of a cultural mountain to actually shift the values represented on that mountain."[83]

This small percentage is the sum total of the true decision makers in education. That means that we as believers let the top 5 percent of the over 3 million people involved in education in this country make all the decisions. The rest of us watch on the sidelines as decisions are made that take our country down a path of socialism and ultimately destruction to the way of life our forefathers intended.

The church has lost its vision for stewarding the territory God given us. We has have allowed the voice of God to be muffled as Goliath taunted us day after day. Christian teachers in the classroom have their hands tied because of the lack of prayer by apostolic prayer teams who know how to release the power of God in worship, intercession, authority of the Name of Jesus, and strategic warfare.

We have a purpose: to manifest God's Kingdom on the earth today. In the past we have lost ground, but we can regain it if we fight. In her book, *Don't Let the Kids Drink the Kool-Aid*, Mary Beth Hicks wrote:

"In 2007, while still a member of the United States Senate, Barack Obama said, 'I am absolutely convinced that culture wars are just so '90s. Their days are growing dark.' Obama was right. The culture wars are over: We lost. We are no longer fighting to uphold traditional social values. Now we're fighting a battle over the very definition of what it means to be an American, and what America means to the world. A losing battle."[84]

I would say that Hicks is right—except that God is calling His people to come together to pray in a strategic way as never before in the history of the world. Kingdom-minded people are being called into place. We must follow the instructions the prophet Joel gave his warriors, "Do not break ranks." (Joel 2:8.)

Until we are called by someone with an apostolic jurisdiction we do not know how to stand together and not break ranks. The apostle puts prayer warriors in position and gives the orders and teaches them how to stand together without breaking ranks. With such a dynamic prayer team, we can take back our educational system as well as the other cultural influences in our nation.

40 The Sound of Victory

Our educational system is poised for great changes. Those of us who are not directly involved with education as a parent, student, or administrator, do not have firsthand knowledge of how dangerously close we are to implosion. Only when the news broadcasts the most recent school shooting do we get a jolt reminding us that our system is broken. The brilliant minds that rule the halls of academics have no clue how to fix it. Only God can repair what is horribly broken and only those who know a powerful God and who are willing to stand in the gap on behalf of the children in our schools can see it repaired.

If we listen closely, we will hear some of the solutions that are being posed. Presently there are a tremendous number of charter schools being founded. Public schools do not necessarily like charter schools. Charter schools take money and resources from public schools and consequently are seen as diversions. Many parents dislike them because they do not educate all the students in an area. A charter school can siphon off the brightest students and educate them apart from the masses. Although anyone can apply to a charter school, most likely only the top students will be accepted.

Another rustling on the horizon is what educational project foundations will underwrite. Recently in a TV interview, Paul Tudor Jones, the founder of Robin Hood Foundation, said, **"The only way to combat poverty in America is to completely revise our educational system."** Jones knows education firsthand. Once a hedge fund manager, he has raised billions of dollars through his Robin Hood Foundation to be given to schools in America. His observation that the current system isn't working should be a clue to every prayer warrior in the country that it is time for God to raise up a new foundation for our educational system.

In 2 Samuel 5:23–24, David asked the Lord how to advance against the Philistine army. The Lord replied, **"Do not go straight up, but circle around behind them and attack them in front of the balsam trees. As soon as you hear the sound of marching in the tops of the balsam trees, move quickly because that will mean the LORD has gone out in front of you."**

When we hear reports that our educational system needs a complete makeover, then it is time to march around behind them, take our spiritual position, and pray for God to do something new in our country. Do you hear the rustling in the tops of the balsam trees? If so, it is time to pray.

I find strength for battle not only in the Bible, but through natural wars that have been fought and won. One of my favorite places in Washington, DC is the Korean War Memorial. During my first visit to the site I felt as though I were walking on hallowed ground. The memorial consists of nineteen statues of men dressed in full combat gear walking through a muddy field. The sense of determination and purpose engraved on their faces.

After taking a slight turn at the memorial, I found myself at a shallow circular pool about thirty feet in diameter, called the Pool of Remembrance. Along the edge of the pool were the Korean War statistics—the number of people killed, wounded, missing in action, and prisoners of war. That data alone is moving, but another inscription moved my heart: **"Our nation honors her sons and daughters who answered the call to defend a country they never knew and a people they never met."**

When we bow our knees in prayer for those whom we will never know and never meet on earth, we have entered hallowed ground. Intercessors most likely will never experience the physical hardships the troops endured, but we certainly know the calling to give ourselves to defend the Kingdom of God by praying for people in distant lands and, in our case, in our schools and in organizations which we may never enter.

Anyone who takes on the challenge to pray for America's schools will walk that same path. While we may never know the students, teachers, and organizations, we certainly know that we have a mission of redemption for the millions of children who are caught in a battle that if we lose will result in the downfall of this country. It's a somber challenge for us.

41 Pray for America's Schools Like You Pray for a Sick Friend

Many people are very concerned for the future of our children and our schools but feel that it is only a matter of time until our educational system will fail. I've had my finger on the pulse of this system for years and I can tell you this: **Our Educational System is in a Critical Condition.** That's why so many people say, "Why bother to pray for education?" They talk about how the Lord's return is so near, and how things are just going to get worse and worse before Jesus comes back to earth and rescues us. End of discussion. They continue to worry and look for the Rapture. In my opinion, those negative comments and that longing look for redemption in the form of the Rapture are a cover-up for lack of faith and prayer.

I agree that our educational system appears terminal. But how would those of us who are supposed to be faith-filled believers react if we had a good friend who had fallen into sin and become sick? What if that person had turned his back on God? What if you knew that if that person regained his health he could change this nation? What if that person's friends had all turned against him and refused to pray? What if that person had been exploited by people who had taken advantage of him? What if that person had provided for the education of hundreds of thousands of children throughout the world and would do so again, when he recovered? What if you knew that that friend, when recovered, would engage in even greater humanitarian acts than he had ever done before? Would you pray for them? Yes, every one of us would pray for such a friend. America's educational system is that friend who needs our prayers for health and healing.

Now is not the time to turn against our schools and the education of our children and watch the educational system go downhill. This is the time to rise up in faith and believe God for healing and transformation. We have the opportunity to change this nation and the lives of our children and our children's children for generations to come.

Appendix A: Baal Divorce Decree

THE HIGHEST COURT
OF THE KINGDOM OF GOD

IN RE THE MARRIAGE OF:

THE PEOPLE OF GOD,

    Plaintiff, vs. THE PRINCIPALITY OF BAAL

(Including Baal, Queen of Heaven, Leviathan) Defendant,

<u>**DECREE OF DIVORCE***</u>

This matter comes on for hearing before the Supreme Judge of the Highest Court of the Kingdom of God on the petition of The People of God seeking a Decree of Divorce from The Principality of Baal, the Defendant in this matter.

The Court finds:

    The Plaintiff's assertions are fully substantiated:

        That this marriage was entered into by the Plaintiff based on lies and deceit by the Defendant, and

        That Plaintiff relied on fraudulent inducements and enticements by the Defendant, which Defendant had neither the intention or ability to deliver

    The Plaintiff renounces any and all right, claim, or interest in any possession jointly acquired with the Defendant during this Marriage, and that Plaintiff is entitled to have sole right, claim, and interest, in and to all the gifts, possessions and inheritance from Plaintiff's Father, and the Defendant is to be and forever barred from the title, control, or use of any such gifts, possessions or inheritance.

    That all offspring of the marriage have been stillborn or have had viability for only brief periods and were either destroyed by the Defendant or were so infected by sickness attributed to the Defendant's condition that no life remained in them.

    The Plaintiff repudiates any and all joint claims with the Defendant, and requests this court to sever all relationships with the Defendant of any nature, however and whenever such occurred,

and seeks enforcement by this Court of Plaintiff's desire to be
known by no other name than that given by Plaintiff's Father.

The Plaintiff also seeks an everlasting restraining order against the
Defendant so as to keep the Defendant away from all persons or
property belonging to the Plaintiff.

THE JUDGEMENT

WHEREFORE, this Court being fully advised in the evidence does find
for the Plaintiff and against the Defendant in all matters material to the
Plaintiff's Petition of Divorce, and does by this decree grant the Plaintiff
a Divorce and all requests set forth above.

That being the Order of this Court, from and after this date, so shall it be.

THE SUPREME JUDGE

* Composed by Dr. Jerry Mash (Oklahoma Apostolic Prayer Network)

For Additional Information:

Dr. John Benefiel, Apostolic Coordinator
Heartland Apostolic Prayer Network
P.O. Box 720006
Oklahoma City, OK 73172
Phone: 405-943-2484 Ÿ Fax: 405-749-0345
Website: www.hapn.us or www.cotr.tv
Email: assistant@hapn.us

Endnotes

CHAPTER 2: HOW BAD IS IT?

[1] Information obtained from cdc.gov/TeenPregnancy/AboutTeenPreg.htm.

[2] National Center for Education Statistics, available from http://nces.ed.gov/programs/crimeindicators/crimeindicators2012/ind_02.asp].

[3] Statistics were taken from http://www.dosomething.org/tipsandtools/background-gang-violence#.

[4] Ben Chapman, *New York Daily News*, "Violent gangs, prostitution, dangerous weapons—in the classroom: Shocking safety agents lawsuit paints deplorable portrait of city schools," March 3, 2013, available from http://www.nydailynews.com/new-york/prostitution-violent-gangs-weapons-city-school-halls-safety-agent-suit-article-1.1278515.

[5] Cheryl Wetzstein, *The Washington Times*, "California transgender 'bathroom law' one step closer to ballot," January 8, 2014, available from http://www.washingtontimes.com/news/2014/jan/8/california-transgender-bathroom-law-one-step-close.

[6] This information was taken from StopTheShootings.org, "Our National Issue," by David Hemenway (professor of Health Policy and Director of the Harvard Injury Control Research Center in Boston, MA), available from http://www.stoptheshootings.org. The 494 amount of deaths was derived by adding up the total number of school shootings and deaths state by state.

[7] US Department of Education, "Department of Education Starts Award for 'Green' Schools," April 6, 2011, available from http://www.ed.gov/news/press-releases/department-education-starts-award-green-schools.

[8] Stephen Ceasar, "L.A. Unified misused $158 million in student meal funds," *Los Angeles Times*, February 6, 2013, available from

http://latimesblogs.latimes.com/lanow/2013/02/lausd-lunch-funds.html.

[9] *The Weekly* , February 18, 2013, Vol. 18, No. 22, "School for Scandal," available from http://www.weeklystandard.com/articles/school-scandal_700516.html#, pp. 3–4.

[10] Information was taken from the Statistic Brain web site, from research done by US Department of Education, National Institute of Literacy, research date April 28, 2013, available from http://www.statisticbrain.com/number-of-american-adults-who-cant-read.

[11] Ibid.

[12] Information taken from National Center for Education Statistics, available from http://nces.ed.gov/surveys/pisa, "Program for International Student Assessment; Overview."

[13] Ibid., available from http://nces.ed.gov/fastfacts/display.asp?id=66, "Fast Facts."

[14] Amanda Gardner, "Many Teens Drinking, Taking Drugs During School: Survey," *U.S. News & World Report*, available from http://health.usnews.com/health-news/news/articles/2012/08/22/many-teens-drinking-taking-drugs-during-school-survey.

[15] Information taken from DoSomething.org, "11 Facts About High School Drop Out Rates," available from https://www.dosomething.org/facts/11-facts-about-high-school-dropout-rates.

[16] Information taken from Kids Count Data Center, Data Source: Population Reference Bureau, analysis of data from the US Census Bureau, 2008–2011 American Community Survey, "Teens Ages 16 to 19 Not Attending School and Not Working," available from http://datacenter.kidscount.org/data/tables/5062-teens-ages-16-to-19-not-attending-school-and-not-working?loc=1&loct=2#detailed/1/any/false/868,867,133,38,35/any/11482,11483.

[17]Information obtained from the Centers for Disease Control and Prevention, "Attention-Deficit /Hyperactivity Disorder (ADHD), Data & Statistics, In the United States," available from http://www.cdc.gov/ncbddd/adhd/data.html.

[18]Quote taken from TeenHelp.com, "Statistics and Self-Injury Treatment," available from http://www.teenhelp.com/teen-health/cutting-stats-treatment.html.

[19]Information taken from the Centers for Disease Control and Prevention, http://www.cdc.gov/HealthyYouth/sexualbehaviors.

[20]Anna Schneider, *Inside Schools*, *Your Independent Guide to NYC Public Schools*, available from http://insideschools.org/blog/item/1000703-test-results-7-in-10-nyc-kids-below-grade-level.

[21]Ken Ham, Britt Beemer, and Todd Hillard, *Already Gone* (Green Forrest, AR: Master Books, 2009), 78.

[22]Ibid., 172.

CHAPTER 3: WHAT IS THE MOUNTAIN OF EDUCATION?

[25]**Salons were a popular** "fashionable assemblage of notables (as literary figures, artists, or statesmen) held by custom at the home of a prominent person." *Merriam-Webster Online Dictionary,* copyright © 2014 by Merriam-Webster, Incorporated; available from http://www.merriam-webster.com/dictionary/salon, s.v. "salon."

CHAPTER 4: WHERE DOES CHANGE START?

[26] Viktor Frankl, *Man's Search for Meaning* (Boston, MA: Beacon Press, 2006), 112.

CHAPTER 5: WHY IS OUR EDUCATIONAL SYSTEM UNDER ATTACK?

[27] Kevin Belmonte, *Hero for Humanity: A Biography of William Wilberforce* (Colorado Springs, CO: Navpress, 2002), 178.

CHAPTER 7: IDENTIFYING THE STRONGMAN

[28]Quote taken from an article by Scott Sonner (AP), *Las Vegas Sun*, "Nevada school shooting probe looks at bullying video,"

available from
http://www.lasvegassun.com/news/2013/oct/24/nevada-school-shooting-probe-looks-bullying-video.

CHAPTER 8: ANCIENT THRONES OF INIQUITY

[29]W. E. Vine, Merrill F. Unger, William White, Jr., *Vine's Complete Expository Dictionary of Old and New Testament Words* (Nashville, TN: Thomas Nelson Inc., 1984), 12.

[30]Based on information from *John Gill's Exposition of the Entire Bible*, available from
http://www.biblestudytools.com/commentaries/gills-exposition-of-the-bible/romans-11-4.html, s.v. "To the image of Baal," Romans 11:4.

[31]John Benefiel, *Binding the Strongman Over America* (Oklahoma City, OK: Benefiel Ministries, Inc., 2012), page 37.

CHAPTER 9: THE AGE OF REASON

[32] Abortion Statistics: United States Data and Trends,
http://www.nationalrighttolifenews.org/news/wp-content/uploads/2012/01/statsre.jpg.

[33]Thomas Paine, *The Theological Works of Thomas Paine* (Chicago, IL: Belford, Clark & Company), p 31.

CHAPTER 10: SECULAR EDUCATION

[34] Bob Unruh, *Now School Bans Christmas Carol Melodies,* available from http://www.wnd.com/2013/11/now-school-bans-christmas-carol-melodies/ #E2b9WgEciQJzY1eM.99.

[35]Ayn Rand, *The Virtue of Selfishness* (New York, NY: Penguin Group, 1961), 109.

[36]Peter Wagner, *Warfare Prayer: How to Seek God's Power and Protection in the Battle to Build His Kingdom* (Ventura, CA: Regal Books, 1997), p 1-4.

CHAPTER 12: APOSTOLIC LEADERS

[37] Max Boot, *The Weekly Standard,* December 31, 2012, VOL. 18, NO. 16, *What Wingate Wrought: the astonishing raids of a Special Operations pioneer in Palestine, Abyssinia, and Burma,* available from http://www.jidaily.com/97a8e.

[38]See Judges 7.

[39] Max Boot, *The Weekly Standard*, December 31, 2012, VOL. 18, NO 16, *What Wingate Wrought: the astonishing raids of a Special Operations pioneer in Palestine, Abyssinia, and Burma*, available from http://www.jidaily.com/97a8e.

[40]http://www.charismanews.com/opinion/38897-what-the-church-can-learn-from-starbucks-bold-stance-on-gay-marriage.

[41]Dr. J. Robert Clinton, *The Making of a Leader: Recognizing the Lessons and Stages of Leadership Development* (Colorado Springs, CO: NavPress, 1988), p 57-124.

CHAPTER 13: INFLUENCERS

[42] Joseph John gurney, *Familiar Sketch of the Late William Wilberforce* (Norwich, England: Josiah Fletcher, 1838), p 40.

[43] *The Making of a Leader*, 74.

[44] Porter B. Williamson, *General Patton's Principles for Life & Leadership*, (Tucson, AZ: Management & Systems Consultants, Inc.,1979), p 188.

[45] http://www.charismanews.com/opinion/38897-what-the-church-can-learn-from-starbucks-bold-stance-on-gay-marriage.

[46] Dr. John Benefiel, *Binding the Strongman Over America: Healing the Land, transferring Wealth, and Advancing the Kingdom of God* (Oklahoma City, OK: Benefiel Ministries, Inc.2013), p 23.

CHAPTER 15: THE FORCE OF A FEW

[47] Jack Utter, *American Indians: Answers to today's Questions,* (Lake Ann, MI: National Woodlands Publishing, 1993), 86.

[48]John Steinbeck, *Grapes of Wrath* (New York, NY: The Viking Press/Penguin Group, 2006, revised edition).

[49]Tulsa World, *OKC Mayor Talks about Turnaround Mentality*, Thursday, March 21, 2013, www.tulsaworld.com.

CHAPTER 16: GROUND LEVEL STRATEGIES

[50]Francis Frangipane, *This Day We Fight!* (Ada, MI: Chosen Books,

2010) 100.

[51]James P. Moore, *One Nation Under God: The History of Prayer in America* (New York, NY: Broadway Books, 2007), 377.

[52] http://www.edreform.com/2012/04;k-12-facts/.

[53]Malcolm Gladwell, *The Tipping Point: How Little Things Can Make a Big Difference* (New York City, NY: Back Bay Books, 2002).

CHAPTER 18: NATIVE AMERICANS AND EDUCATION

[54] Information taken from Williams College, *Archives and Special Collections*, "Haystack Celebration Collection, 1815–2007," "Historical Note," available from http://archives.williams.edu/manuscriptguides/haystack/bio.php.

[55] Stan Juneau, *A History and foundation of American Indian Education Policy, Montana State Office of Public Instruction, Helena, MT, 2001, www.opistate.mt.us/PDF/IndPolicyHistory.pdf, pg 23.*

[56] http://nah.org/pdfs/otherislanders/1aWamp2o2.pdf.

CHAPTER 20: ENTRY POINT #1: THE TAKEOVER OF HARVARD

[57] John A. Stormer, *None Dare Call it Education: What's Happening in Our Schools? The documented account of how education "reforms" are undermining academics and traditional values* (Florissant, MO: Liberty Bell Press, 1999), 86.

[58]Samuel Blumenfeld, *NEA: Trojan Horse in American Education* (Boise, Idaho: Paradigm Company, 1984), 8.

[59] Erick Metaxas, general editor, *Socrates in the City: Conversations on "Life, God, and Other Small Topics,"* (New York, NY: Penguin Group, 2011), 122.

[60]*NEA: Trojan Horse in American Education*, 17.

[61]Wayne Urban and Jennings Wagoner, *American Education: A History, Second* Edition (New York, NY: McGraw-Hill Higher Education, 2000), 118.

[62] NEA: *Trojan Horse in American Education*, 16.

CHAPTER 22: ENTRY POINT #3:1892 DECISION TO TURN OVER THE EDUCATION OF CHILDREN TO THE

STATE

[63]Kansas Educators and Kansas State Historical Society, *Columbia History of Education in Kansas* (Topeka, KS: Edwin H. Snow, Senate Printer, 1893), 82.

[64]Quote taken from a speech delivered by Adolf Hitler on November 6, 1933, quoted by William Shirer in his book, *The Rise and Fall of the Third Reich* (New York, NY: Simon & Schuster, 1990), 249.

CHAPTER 23: ENTRY POINT#4: JOHN DEWEY AND WRITING THE HUMANIST MANIFESTO

[65]Humanist Manifesto I and II (Buffalo, NY: Prometheus Books, 1973), 7._[66]

http://www.americanhumanist.org/humanism/Humanist_Manifesto_1.

[67]

http://www.americanhumanist.org/humanism/Humanist_Manifesto_1.

[68] William J. Murray, *My Life Without God: The Rest of the Story*, (Eugene, OR: Harvest House Publishers. 1992), 107-108.

[69]James P. Moore, Jr., *One Nation Under God: The History of Prayer in America* (New York, NY: Doubleday, 2005), 359–361.

[70]*One Nation Under God*, 362–363.

[71]http://ffrf.org/news/news-releases/item/17695-muldrow-public-schools-removes-ten-commandments-postings-from-classrooms

CHAPTER 25: ENTRY POINT #6: THE TEN COMMANDMENTS REMOVED FROM PUBLIC SCHOOLS

[72] Alex Murashko, *The Christian Post*, August 7, 2013, "Cullman County Prayer Caravan Sponsor Not Afraid to Take Stand Against Atheists' Demands," available from ChristianPost.com/news/cullman-county-prayer-caravcan-sponsor-not-afraid-to-take-stand-against-atheists-demands-101706.

CHAPTER 26: ENTRY POINT #7: IT BECOMES UNLAWFUL TO TEACH ANYTHING BUT EVOLUTION

IN PUBLIC SCHOOLS

[73]This quote by Zack Kopplin was taken from the Melissa Harris-Perry Blog, May 1, 2013. She is an author and the host of the MSNBC show, "Melissa Harris-Perry."

[74]*Socrates in the City*, 317.

CHAPTER 27: ENTRY POINT #8: THE NATIONAL EDUCATION ASSOCIATION (NEA)

[75] *NEA: the Trojan Horse of American Education,* 139.

[76]John A. Stormer, *None Dare Call It Education* (Florissant, Missouri: Liberty Bell Press, 1999), 210.

CHAPTER 28: ENTRY POINT #9: POSTMODERNISM AND THE REWRITING OF HISTORY

[77] *My Life Without God: The Rest of the Story*, 64.

[78]Mary Beth Hicks, *Don't Let the Kids Drink the Kool-Aid: Confronting the Left's Assault on Our Families, Faith, and Freedom* (Washington, DC: Regnery Publishing, Inc., 2011), xi.

[79]*Don't Let the Kids Drink the Kool-Aid*, 1.

[80]Rebecca Huval, *Revising the Revisionaries: The Texas Board of Ed Loses Power over Textbooks,* January 24, 2013, on PBS.com, "Independent Lens Blog," available from http://www.pbs.org/independentlens/blog/revising-the-revisionaries-the-texas-board-of-ed-loses-its-power-over-textbooks.

CHAPTER 29: ENTRY POINT #10: NATIONAL DEPARTMENT OF EDUCATION

[81]According to the WallBuilders web site, "WallBuilders is an organization dedicated to presenting America's forgotten history and heroes, with an emphasis on the moral, religious, and constitutional foundation on which America was built"; available from http://www.wallbuilders.com/ABTOverview.asp.

[82] Cornelia "Corrie" ten Boom was a Dutch Christian who, along with her father and other family members, helped many Jews escape the Nazi Holocaust during World War II and was imprisoned for it. Wikipedia

CHAPTER 30: DAVID AND GOLIATH

[83]Os Hillman, *Change Agent: Engaging Your Passion to Be the One Who Makes a Difference* (Lake Mary, FL: Charisma House Book Group, 2011), 8.

[84]*Don't Let the Kids Drink the Kool-Aid*, ix.

ABOUT NANCY HUFF

Nancy Huff has always been in education in some form or another. She taught Jr. High and High School mathematics in public and private schools. She has a B. S. E. in Mathematics and a Master's degree in English as a Second Language. Fifteen years ago she resigned teaching to found Teach the Children International (TCI), a nonprofit organization that reaches out to children at risk in the United States and abroad. Internationally TCI reaches out to refugee children.

TCI sponsored a program called "Take a Walk That Will Change Eternity." Individuals and churches are trained to prayerwalk schools and then adopt that school for the purpose of providing service projects that encourage students, teachers, administrators and support staff. TCI sponsored city-wide call to prayer meetings for schools located in the Tulsa, Oklahoma area. In order to pray for education more effectively, Nancy researched the history of our educational system. This book is an outgrowth of her discoveries.

Along with writing numerous magazine articles, Nancy wrote Safety Zone: Scriptural Prayers to Revolutionize Your School, How to Create Passive Income with Rental Property, and co authored A Call to Prayer for Teens, Children, and Young Adults in the 10/40 Window (WYAM).

Nancy may be contacted at:

Teach The Children International, Inc.
 P. O. Box 700832
Tulsa, OK 74170-0832
(918) 369-5081
E-mail: ContactTCI@aol.com
Web site: NancyHuff.com
Web site: TeachtheChildrenInternatinal.com

Free Prayer Updates

TO EMPOWER YOU TO PRAY FOR TRANSFORMATION IN AMERICAN EDUCATION AND IN YOUR SCHOOL

WHY SUBSCRIBE?

- **Gives You Historical Insight –** Allows you to address root problems in prayer

- **You Receive Prayer Updates –** Address educational issues that are happening right now

- **Keeps You Current on Educational Issues** – So you can educate others on how to pray for our schools.

Sign up at:
TakingTheMountainofEducation.com

Made in the USA
Columbia, SC
22 October 2022

69861205R00143